THE
VALUE
SELLING
ANTHOLOGY

GARY S. TUBRIDY

About Alexander Group:
The Alexander Group (www.alexandergroup.com) provides sales management consulting services to the world's leading sales organizations, serving Global 2000 companies from across all industries. Founded in 1985, Alexander Group combines deep experience, a proven methodology and data-driven insights to help sales leaders anticipate change, align their sales force with company goals and make better informed decisions with one goal in mind—to grow sales. The Alexander Group has offices in Atlanta, Chicago, San Francisco, Scottsdale and Stamford.

Our Consulting Services
The Alexander Group provides the world's leading sales organizations with management consulting services for the full spectrum of sales force needs, as well as compensation analysis and performance benchmarking based on the industry's richest repository of sales data.

We apply years of experience and our Sales Management System™, a proven methodology for evaluating sales organizations, to provide insights that are rooted in facts. We not only deliver insights—we understand sales and marketing business challenges. We roll up our sleeves to work alongside our clients, whether they are slightly realigning their sales coverage model or radically overhauling their sales force. Beyond that, our keen focus on measurement ensures that we deliver value to our clients. And results.

AGI Press

The Value Selling Anthology

ISBN: 978-0-9899480-6-7

This publication is designed to provide accurate and authoritative information in regard to the subject matter covered. It is sold with the understanding that neither the author nor the publisher are engaged in rendering legal, accounting or other professional service. If legal advice or other expert assistance is required, the services of a competent professional person should be sought.

—*From a Declaration of Principles Jointly Adopted by a Committee of the American Bar Association and a Committee of Publishers and Associations.*

For information about this title or to order other books and/or electronic media, contact us at www.alexandergroup.com.

Table of Contents

Acknowledgments

THE VALUE SELLING ANTHOLOGY is a compendium of articles written by many authors and based on the wisdom and experience of many sales executives. I dedicate this book to those who made it possible.

To my colleagues at the Alexander Group who contributed the articles and concepts that made this book possible.

To my partners at the Alexander Group, Dave Cichelli and Bob Conti, whose support I can always count on.

To the many clients and friends who contributed their intellectual capital to advance the art of value selling.

And to my wife, Erica, and my daughters, Laura, Elizabeth and Catherine, who make anything possible and everything a joy.

Introduction

The Value Selling Anthology

The prominence and importance of the sales function are rising. Why? And what does that mean for sales leaders?

While other functions have been frozen or even diminished as a result of the 2008 recession, the sales function has been the least affected overall and, in many companies, is now even thriving. Companies that invest in the sales function understand two things:

1. The sales function is the focal point for delivering value to the customer. Sellers discover the issues and marshal the resources to solve problems for customers. If the company cares about its reputation, its position in the market and its future, it must also care about the sales function.

2. The sales function is a hugely important conduit of information between the market and the company. As value is delivered through sales, companies also gather information and strategic insight from their best customers about what matters most to them.

Intuitively, most companies know that it is not wise to cut back on this type of resource. Consider the statistics pulled from the Alexander Group's *Sales Pulse Survey* (run annually for the past decade) from post-recession 2009 to the present:

YEAR	2009	2010	2011	2012	2013
Median Projected Revenue Growth	6.7%	7%	6%	7.5%	6%
Median Projected Headcount Growth	2%	2%	1%	1%	2%

The *Sales Pulse Survey* focuses primarily on Fortune 1000-size companies with about 110 participants per year. Note that the median sales growth goal in each year markedly exceeds gross domestic product growth…usually by a factor of about 3X. Note too that for the sales function:

- Modest growth in headcount is projected each year, but…
- Headcount growth substantially lags expected revenue growth.

This is not a "business-as-usual" situation. Aggressive revenue growth expectations are forcing sales executives to be more productive, and to do more with less. These executives cannot buy growth with more headcount, so they need to find ways to get more output from their current headcount. This is no easy course to steer. It is driving many companies to consider both the size of the customers they are targeting, as well as how these customers buy and what they value. The basic choices faced are illustrated in the following graphic:

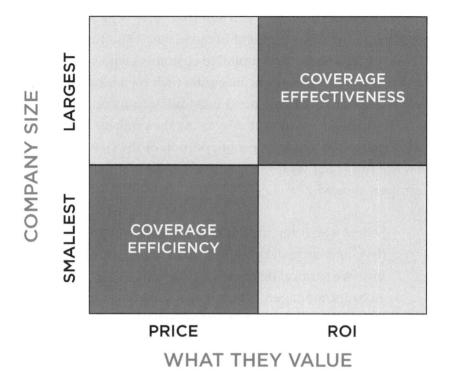

By considering *what* customers value in addition to *how much* they buy, companies are increasingly making the choice between maximizing coverage *effectiveness* vs. coverage *efficiency*. Where efficiency is needed because of tight margins and procurement-driven RFPs, alternate channels such as the Web, partners and inside sales will play a much larger role in minimizing the cost of covering low-margin segments. When customers value the ROI on what they are purchasing, there is often willingness to pay a premium because the relationship with the vendor leads to better outcomes in either spending, revenue or both. In such situations, investment in sales talent that can build a case to purchase based on ROI and maintain relationships that are founded on value is a wise choice. How such choices are made is the focus of this *Value Selling Anthology*.

In this *Anthology*, you will see that sales organizations are investing in the value segment because they want their sellers to deliver critical intellectual capital to customers who are willing to pay for it. As these customers encounter their own fiscal challenges, they are seeking ways to spend less and earn more. Sellers who can help them achieve this goal by using the products and services they represent to better run some portion of the customer's business are rewarded with increasing share and/or better margins. Examples abound...

- Sellers who listen to physician needs team up with product development to design and market high-margin, minimally invasive surgical devices.
- Account managers who observe inventory management techniques at a customer and suggest process changes that can save millions build both share and margin.
- Account executives team up with field marketing to help a retail partner better promote its premium products leading to improved revenue and margin for both.

The common denominator across all these examples is a seller who, alone or with a team, figures out a way to help his/her customer earn more money. That is, they deliver value beyond the characteristics of the products they sell. As one executive stated, "Competitors can copy our products, but they can't easily imitate the value we deliver through our sellers. Value through people is something you have to build from the ground up; there are no shortcuts."

That is what this *Value Anthology* is all about...articulating what companies are doing to pivot their sales organizations away from pushing products to delivering value. You will see that such customer-motivated sales organizations tend to have four things in common. They...

Inspire

Sales leaders find ways to offer their sellers the opportunity to be part of something big. They inspire their sellers to deliver value to the customer as part of a mission to improve both the business and something approaching the noble pursuit of improving society. For healthcare companies that is not too big a leap...bring new products and technologies to market faster and improve or even save lives. But this too goes for companies in other industries. Building products companies promote their ability to help customers consume less energy. Software, hardware and cloud companies speak to their ability to help the world stay connected. Logistics companies help customers deliver product, sometimes life-saving, to remote locations. No, sellers are not expected to be altruistic. There is and should be good compensation and lifestyle attached to being a part of such an organization. But such elements are secondary or even tertiary to the expressed mission of helping customers thrive and in the process make someone's life just a bit better. Selling is a noble profession in these companies.

Innovate

"Healthy paranoia" means never being satisfied with the status quo. Sales executives in the most successful contemporary sales organizations will not rest on their laurels; they will always be looking for a better way. After achieving 105 percent of goal one year, they will ask: "What must we do differently to deliver even better results next year?" In a word, such organizations and the executives who run them are "innovative." They seek out different approaches, experiment all the time and accept change willingly because they know the ability to change and adapt keeps them ahead of the evolutionary curve. They will test the usefulness of specialists and introduce them rapidly if proven effective. Eighteen months later they will be testing for when these same specialists can be discontinued and the investment redeployed to a new growth opportunity. These executives and the organizations they run are agile, willing to test for a better way to operate and quick to change when something new is proven to work. And, equally important, they are willing to forgive well-meaning initiatives that fail, which were undertaken in the interest of finding a better way.

Focus

Expectations for revenue growth have been outpacing the growth in sales headcount. The only way to grow fast under these conditions is to focus your resources where they will make the most difference…in account segments that are growing or that place a premium on value. That sounds easy enough but is often difficult to pull off in practice. Relationship selling often needs to be challenged when accounts turn over buying processes to procurement, demand deep discounts and refuse to place value on expertise you can provide. This is especially true of extremely large accounts that morph into what some call "RFP bullies," which expect break-even pricing in exchange for large orders. Where this is true, should you decide to do business at all, coverage efficiency is the key using inside sales and the Internet to fulfill demand. Value selling is all about stimulating demand and serving customer needs with expensive expertise. Focus means finding out where these accounts are. This requires both new segmentation techniques and a willingness to change coverage patterns to reach accounts that warrant more expensive coverage.

Invest

In most organizations, planned investment lags the expected rate of growth. But for companies that are strategically positioning themselves in the value-selling segment, investment in the sales force is much more aggressive. Per the *2013 Sales Pulse Survey*, these organizations are expected to deliver growth that is two times the median (12 percent vs. 6 percent). To accomplish this, these same organizations are ramping up their investment in sales resources at a much higher rate. They are growing...

- Field sales resources at a rate of 6 percent vs. the median of 2 percent.
- Inside sales resources 1.6X faster than the median.
- Sales operations resources 3X faster than the median.

That means more feet on the street, more specialists, more managers to coach, more tools and better sales operations functions to make all of this investment more productive. These organizations plan to deliver significant resources to the accounts that will value it most.

Sales leaders have never been better positioned to influence the strategies and the results of the companies at which they work. These leaders are moving from a purely tactical platform (take the numbers and run) to a strategic platform that affords influence on products, investments and marketing, as well as sales strategies. It means that top sales executives need to find a path to the planning table to get a stronger voice in the decisions that influence the outcomes of the business. That is happening naturally in many businesses, but not all. Where the sales function remains an implementation tool, general management, marketing and financial management need to be awakened to the perils of this point of view. Time for sales to get a seat at the planning table!

What does this mean for sales leaders?

Sales leaders must take steps to build value-based sales resources of their own. To do this, they will need answers to four critical questions:

1. How can sales play a role, perhaps a leading one, in the mission to serve customers who are willing to pay a premium for value delivered?
2. How can a sales executive make the case for investment in value-based selling?
3. What is the roadmap for implementing a value-based sales strategy?
4. How do you prepare sales resources for the transformation journey?

During the past three years, the Alexander Group has conducted dozens of surveys and scores of interviews to get answers to these very questions. A partial list of the companies whose executives contributed ideas, observations and quotes to this research is in the Appendix. This research has over time been converted into articles and white papers covering multiple aspects of value selling...from creating a vision to implementing it. This *Anthology* accumulates all these articles in one place and organizes them in a way that we hope will be useful to sales leaders. It is divided into five sections:

SECTION	DESCRIPTION
I. A New Role for Sales	Explores the rising strategic importance of the sales function as sellers add value to products and services by imbedding intellectual capital and expertise into the sales process.
II. Customer-Motivated Selling	Describes what leading sales forces are doing to pivot from selling "things" to solving problems for customers by suggesting innovative ways to use the products and services they offer.
III. Strategic Investment in Sales	Describes how to make the financial case for investing in sales resources that deliver profitable growth by adding value to the products they promote.
IV. Provisioning for Value	Articulates the resources, programs and tools needed to deliver value through sales.
V. Charting the Course to Value	Offers guidance on how to ready the sales force for a culture that puts customer success ahead of pushing products.

If adding value through sales is a part of your growth strategy, this *Anthology* will be of great value to you. We hope you enjoy it and profit from it.

SECTION I

A New Role for Sales

A New Role for Sales

IT IS HARD, IF NOT IMPOSSIBLE, to consistently differentiate your company and command premium prices based on product excellence alone. Too many competitors are adept at copying product features, and dropping price to attract attention and secure fast if less profitable revenue. One executive noted, "Competitors can copy my product. But they cannot easily copy the value we deliver with our sales force and the processes we have crafted by hand." Expanding on this wisdom, many companies have come to recognize the power of using the sales force as a means to beat the competition the old-fashioned way...deliver a better proposition to the customer by combining products with the wisdom and expertise of the sales function to solve problems. Thus, a new role for sales and a more expansive opportunity for the sales function is emerging.

ARTICLES IN THIS SECTION

- New Rules: Bold Solutions
- How Companies Use Their Sales Force to Outmaneuver the Competition in a Slow Growth Economy
- Better Results Through Value Selling

Chapter 1

New Rules: Bold Solutions

Author:
Gary S. Tubridy
Senior Vice President
The Alexander Group, Inc.

AT TWO RECENT Regional Chief Sales Executive (CSE) Forums, more than 70 executives gathered to explore bold solutions and new sales roles that are being implemented by sales leaders to stimulate solid growth in an indifferent economy by delivering more value to increasingly sophisticated customers.

The Challenge

Sales leaders at the Spring CSE Forums recognized the central roles of their sales forces in capturing growth in an indifferent economy. They know that when the economy is tight, good selling can inspire customers to shift some share of their business to vendors that offer more value.

Most contemporary growth plans revolve around the sales force delivering greater value. In the Alexander Group's *2012 Sales Pulse*

Survey, customer-centric, value-oriented strategies predominated among the highest growth companies.

Sales Strategies Are Dependent on Growth Aspirations

The problem is, building a value strategy is easier than executing one. CSE Forum guests cited three primary factors:

1. *Most sales forces are more comfortable in "show-and-tell" mode when selling their products and services.* Lacking good understanding or perspective on how products and services can be configured and used by clients to improve business results, most sellers simply push product features. This opens them up to ferocious price competition when there are functionally equivalent products on the market. To combat this, salespeople and processes need an infusion of business acumen.

2. *Most selling is targeted at traditional buyers...mid-level managers with whom the seller is comfortable and familiar.* In today's world, commodity transactions are being taken over by procurement...and run like an auction where the best price wins. If you want to sell value and vision (at a premium), you need to reach C-suite executives with messages that will resonate with them.

3. *Growth cannot be achieved by focusing primarily on current accounts.* Sellers must spark the interest of accounts that currently purchase little or nothing from them. They have to go where the growth opportunities lie. Yet, Alexander Group research indicates that 75 percent of seller time is typically devoted to servicing current accounts and traditional buyers. Forum executives agree that this is "no way to ramp up growth."

Stepping Up

What must be done? Following are the steps that Forum executives identified as necessary to drive sales growth in a time when value is the name of the game and investment resources are hard to come by.

Improved processes—a more explicit sales strategy planning process. Companies launch new products and services frequently. They acquire new companies and expand their capabilities in the interest of enriching the value of what they can offer to the customer. What does this mean to the sales force and how it must behave? Companies need to explicitly identify not only the segments they are targeting but the accounts at which incremental growth ambitions can be achieved. This includes both accounts that can be further penetrated, as well as accounts that can be won from the competition.

More sophisticated selling behavior directed at important new buying audiences. Sellers will need to execute different sales modes to effectively represent new services and sell value to increasingly important C-suite buyers. Stand-alone product promotion on the basis of "feeds and speeds" is not adequate for buyers who own responsibility for processes and functions. New modes where sellers educate customers on new capabilities, partner on possible solutions to business issues and show vision on how to use enriched services to better compete are now needed. If products cannot be shown to impact results, then they are by definition a commodity and subject to price pressure at the procurement level.

New sales processes employing multiple resources at different times are likely to be needed. None of this can be left to chance...it needs clear articulation and provisioning.

Smart investments. Add value where it counts. Focus limited investment dollars where there is the greatest chance of a return...on customers of a size and inclination to pay for value. Such investment can include:

- Time and resources devoted to more in-depth discovery with customer leadership.
- Tools and resources to produce sophisticated solution configurations.
- Implementation plans and ROI assessments.

This requires real resources and real investment to pull off. Most executives agreed that they cannot afford this in all segments, but need to target such investment on segments that offer payback. A partnership with marketing to help identify these account segments moves from "nice to have" to necessity.

Drive efficiency where you must. To pay for investment in delivering value at accounts that are willing to pay for it, executives pointed to the need for greater coverage efficiency among accounts that are more oriented to purchasing on the basis of price or that do not buy enough product/service to warrant premium coverage. Expensive field-based sellers are a cost that can no longer be borne at such accounts. These executives suggest covering price-oriented customers with some combination of inside sales and Web-based solutions. Consider using partners where customers desire value, but do not have the scale to buy in quantity. Or consider inside/outside sales partnering where inside sellers identify the opportunities and outside specialists do targeted and very efficient follow up.

In all cases, shift administrative and service tasks to less expensive resources to free up expensive selling resources to focus on non-routine, high-value activities.

Courage to Change (and Sometimes Fail)

Change from a position of strength, not desperation. When sales flatten and profit pressures mount, top sales executives suggest that it is time for bold moves, something different. It is definitely *not* time for "wait and see." It is better not to be caught flatfooted. Try new approaches in search of better ways to improve efficiency or to add value. Run lots of pilots. Find what does not work…and scrap it. Find what does work…and scale it. Change is hard business; it is the leader's job to make his or her organization "change friendly." Sales leadership is not just about great execution. It is about innovating, testing, scaling and growing. And tolerating occasional well-intentioned failures that are bound to occur when field managers try new approaches to meeting customer needs and adding value.

Change people too if they are unable or unwilling to accept a new imperative. Even if (perhaps especially if) they are former stars, some salespeople simply need to go. Executives indicate that upwards of 50 percent eventually leave during transformation. This will include those who cannot, as well as those who will not, adopt new sales modes. Do not delay the inevitable. Show those who are willing to change that you are serious by taking swift action against those who hold out or refuse to change. Don't back away from the people challenge…lean in.

For those who choose change, be willing to work with them. Some get it right away. For many, it will take time and coaching. Make it clear that, for those who are willing to put in the effort, you are willing to put in the time. No, it is not a ticket to perpetual non-performance. But for those who are trying hard, allow them the time to turn the corner on the road to success.

Closing Comments

It looks like 2013 is set to be another "interesting" year. According to early findings from the *2013 Sales Pulse Survey*, median sales growth of 5 percent is expected. Yet, according to most economists, the gross domestic product will likely not exceed 1.5 percent growth. And, according to the *Sales Pulse Survey,* median investment in sales resources next year will grow by only 2.5 percent. The executives at the Spring Forums told us that they will not make their numbers next year through "business as usual." There are indeed new rules for sales. Executives will blend investments in selling value with initiatives to better manage the cost of sales coverage. The plan is to combine bold coverage solutions with enhanced efficiency to meet both ambitious growth and profit objectives. Those sales leaders with a prominent seat at the strategic planning table will be best positioned to pull this off.

Chapter 2

How Companies Use Their Sales Force to Outmaneuver the Competition in a Slow Growth Economy

Author:
Gary S. Tubridy
Senior Vice President
The Alexander Group, Inc.

RECENTLY, THE ALEXANDER GROUP convened three executive roundtables at the Chief Sales Executive Summit. Eighteen top sales executives discussed the critical role of the sales organization in meeting tough growth goals in a difficult economy by adding value to the products and services they sell. Following are highlights and insights gathered from these sessions.

Revenue growth ambition without corresponding growth in headcount means better productivity will be the key to making the numbers.

With gross domestic product (GDP) growth sluggish for the foreseeable future, this situation is likely to continue. Spending will be tight for years to come. Companies will invest cautiously and only in areas linked to their strategic growth plan. Double-digit growth will be fought for and won by carefully targeting opportunity and taking share from competitors. In such an environment, the role of an efficient, focused sales force is critical.

If we heard one thing at the Summits, it was this, "If you expect to sell more, you better plan on selling differently." Executives highlighted the need to tackle the complexity of selling larger deals involving systems of products and services. They cited the need to leverage deep insight into business processes to position these complex systems as "solutions" to the challenges that matter most to their customers.

Solution selling is not new. But mastery of it is rare. During the past 10 years, a decade in which we experienced two major recessions, certain companies have consistently outgrown their competition. They have done so in no small part through a commitment to delivering value to their customers. At the 2010 Spring Summits, we explored how select companies use solution selling to deliver such value, maintain their sales base through lean times and position for growth in the boom years to follow. This executive summary describes four imperatives of sales excellence that can position your company to deliver the value needed to survive and grow in this challenging, post-recession economy:

- Sellers drive sustainable growth when they deliver intellectual property.
- Science is helping shape today's high-impact sales organization.
- The sales function generates innovation that leads to competitive advantage.
- Sellers step up to daunting challenges and growth imperatives when leadership speaks clearly and "carries a big carrot."

Sellers Drive Growth when Delivering Intellectual Property

Sellers deliver the greatest value when they offer insight into how products and services can help customers achieve their business objectives. This approach diverges from the traditional role of delivering product specs. In a slow growth world, amidst hungry competitors, executives know that decisions on which vendors to partner with can have a major impact on their performance. This is particularly true at larger accounts that are subject to greater process complexity. Consider the account segmentation framework in the following image, which describes the role of the seller where:

- Customers range in size from small to large.
- Products/services purchased range from simple to complex.

	SIMPLE	COMPLEX
LARGE	**EMPHASIZE:** Efficient relationship building; consider teaming account managers with tele-resources	**EMPHASIZE:** Account managers who leverage deep account insight and specialist teams to deliver solutions
SMALL	**EMPHASIZE:** Alternatives to direct sales model to improve coverage efficiency and effectiveness	**EMPHASIZE:** Ways to efficiently target expertise via tele, the web or partners

CUSTOMER SIZE

PRODUCTS/SERVICES PURCHASED

Lesson one from the Summits is that where you choose to inject value is critically important. Suppliers should target accounts that can truly benefit from the intellectual property they have to deliver. Solution selling is account sensitive...not everyone needs or wants it. As one executive stated, "Sellers have to provide a vision of where they can help take the client company and how their solutions will help them get there. It is important to sell this proposition to the C-suite; procurement is not interested in value." Focus expensive resources where they have a chance to impact growth and profit. Sharpen efficiency in covering other segments where solutions are less valued.

Delivering at a profit requires proper balance between intellectual product generalist sales talent and specialists. What then is the role of the account manager? As a rule, the term generalist no longer describes the responsibilities of the typical account manager. Historically, generalists handled relationships, but when it came to the details they were quick to call in the appropriate specialist. As the premium on intellectual product rises, this is changing. Said one executive, "Account managers need to know how to sell product that directly affects client work flow. They need the domain expertise to know how the customer will use the product to get the most value from it."

Thus, the role of the account manager is being enriched in several ways:

- They are hunters...they need to be savvy enough about their customers' business to spot opportunities to add value. They also need to know the right executives to help identify and sanction these opportunities.
- They are specialists...they need to know enough about their products and services to credibly dialog with client executives without the need to resort immediately to a specialist. As one executive reported, "The account managers need to get the ball past mid-field. They can't simply hand it off on

their own 20-yard line." In some companies, every account manager must "declare a major," becoming a specialist in something that is pertinent to the accounts they manage. In this way, they deliver more value and better understand how and when to bring in other specialists.

- They are businesspeople...they help their customers assess options based on expected impact to the bottom line and the business plan. They achieve deep understanding of the customers' business model and complexities, which they use to actively identify ways to add value. They participate with specialists in designing workable solutions to complex issues. At the highest level, such sellers achieve the status of trusted advisor. As one executive noted, "These folks approach their relationships with a long-term vision and aim to give their customers the best advice they can to help them achieve their business objectives."

The term generalist today refers more to the breadth of the sellers' responsibilities as opposed to their capabilities, which are deeper than ever. Gone are the days when, as one executive described, "You picked the guy in the 42-long suit and made him the salesperson." Today's seller combines a deep understanding of customer business issues with a practical understanding of their products/services, which, when focused on accounts and executives who value solutions, delivers sustainable growth.

Science Helps Shape High-Impact Sales Organizations

Data and analytics are helping to forge a new strategic capability and operating cadence among today's high-impact sales organizations. This is being driven by a new and fruitful alliance with marketing and the continuing operations.

The emerging relationship between marketing and sales in high-performance organizations...a partnership between peers. Things are changing in the relationship between marketing and sales. Consider their relative roles as described in a typical marketing textbook:

Marketing: "Determines the needs and wants of target markets and adapts the organization to delivering desirable products/services more effectively and efficiently than the competition."

Sales: "A function designed around the assumption that customers will not buy a product or service unless a significant effort is made to stimulate interest and need."

In other words, sellers provide the push behind products that don't sell themselves. And marketing, done right, minimizes the need for sellers in the first place.

If this were ever true, it certainly is not so in the contemporary world of B2B sales and marketing. At the 2010 Spring Summits, we heard about sales organizations that:

- Work with marketing to identify specific customer segments that have like issues and needs for particular solutions…and real growth potential.
- Build specialist expertise (with funding assistance from marketing) in particular products/services/industries to help fashion business solutions to customer issues.
- Work with customers to refine installed solutions and identify opportunities for additional ones to provide valuable and unvarnished feedback to marketing.

Sales and marketing team up to create and deliver value by designing services in the context of customer needs instead of considering customers in the context of product features. Far from pushing unwanted product, latter-day sellers manage intellectual capital

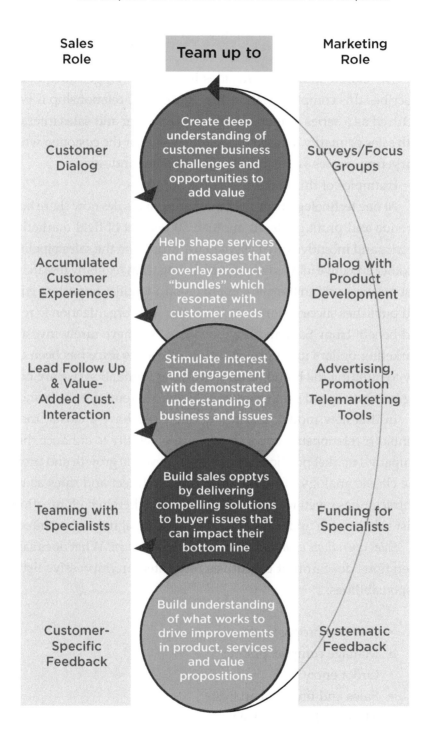

to help deliver meaningful solutions to real business problems that help customers increase revenue, decrease cost or both.

The classic marketing to sales handoff no longer adequately describes this complex relationship. Rather, the relationship is best pictured as a series of loops in which marketing and sales interact, with sales primarily focused on creating value for the customer while marketing creates value for *both* the customer and sales.

Examples of this abounded at the Summits.

At one technology firm, field marketing and sales now share both revenue and profit goals. At another, 50 percent of field marketing metrics and incentives are weighted toward filling the sales pipeline. Another executive told us how the marketing team regularly researches best practices within the sales organization, identifies important wins and publishes success stories for the entire sales organization to read and benefit from. Said another executive, "We have rarely invested marketing dollars into pure branding. The sales force has been the key to building the brand. With that strong foundation, we are now beginning to spend some marketing dollars to reinforce the brand."

In this new model, marketing and sales have a closer, more symbiotic relationship and a shared responsibility to enhance their company's market position, market share, revenue growth and profit. The classic analogy of marketing as the architect and sales as the contractor has given way to a new paradigm wherein both functions exist side-by-side under the roof of a single design-build architect.

Sales operations enables strategic sales management. What does sales operations do? Summit executives recounted an impressive list of responsibilities:

- Develop proposals
- Manage complex pricing
- Order entry
- Sales and financial analysis
- Manage the CRM system

- Sales performance reporting and dashboards
- Maintenance of the customer master file
- Liaison with the marketing team
- Compensation plan administration
- Territory design and maintenance
- Sales process design and tuning
- Sales tool design and tuning

Said one executive, "Our sales ops team has identified the 10 major levers of sales performance. They help us determine which levers to pull to maximize our performance at any given time." Put even more simply, another said, "Ops enables sellers to sell."

This last comment was explored in more depth. What exactly does sales ops do to enable "sellers to sell?" Feedback centered on a common theme: Using data and analytical horsepower, sales ops helps sellers efficiently focus more time and resource on the best targets of opportunity. Sales ops:

- Teams with marketing to identify high-opportunity customer segments.
- Determines which resources to deploy against these opportunities.
- Takes routine tasks off the sellers' plates so they can devote more time to customer-facing activities.
- Supports post-sale implementation to ensure promised productivity gains and ROI are realized by the customer.

Maybe one executive said it best with this comment: "Sales ops is the glue that brings sales and marketing together in a way that produces more value for the company and more value for the customer." Not a bad attribute in an era when sales organization growth depends on how much value you and your organization can bring to the table.

Innovation Leads to Competitive Advantage

Top sales organizations don't wait for performance to crash before making hasty and sometimes ill-considered change. They encourage innovation among their sellers, seeking ideas for new and improved products and processes from the bottom up. They bake this search for improvement into their culture. Reported one executive, "We encourage loud mistakes." They want their sellers to try new approaches "in the interest of serving customers." They know that the price of innovation is the occasional mistake. They also know that the best thinking about how to serve customers, about how to win more business, comes from the field, not headquarters.

Among the executives at the Summits, the value of field-driven innovation was a given. Describing the contribution of field sellers to his product portfolio, one executive told us, "Our sellers worked with marketing to come up with a service that combined convenience and huge time savings for customers. We were immediately able to sell it at a premium. Sales was the driver here; without their insight, no new service." Another executive cited the role of sellers in providing the intellectual leadership to develop unique banking products specifically designed to serve the Islamic world consistent with religious beliefs and culture. There were "on-the-ground" sellers looking for opportunity to meet unique customer needs and grow the business.

How do organizations actually find these great ideas? Programs to harvest great thinking from the field were impressive:

- Many participants create sales councils charged with bringing fresh ideas from the field back to HQ.
- Several participants indicated that they have automated the idea harvesting process. Sellers can phone or write to HQ and ideas are automatically logged, reviewed and prioritized.
- Great stock was put into the personal touch, with several executives touting the value of informal get-togethers between

sales leaders and top performers to gain greater insight into what works and how processes could be improved.

- One participant has instituted a process known as "test and learns" wherein good process ideas are implemented on a limited scale to determine their value and implementation limits. Mistakes are caught early and discarded. Winning ideas are also caught along with hands-on knowledge of how to scale them quickly.

Ideas flowing out of such harvesting efforts were many and impressive. One executive described how his sellers suggested offloading routine post-sale service onto a pre-existing telecoverage organization, resulting in a 10 percent increase in available sales time. Said he, "With people-intensive processes, you must continually try to identify and leverage best practices." Another described how one region began to routinely call in top headquarters executives to participate in region-based user group meetings to hear directly from customers about what was working and what was not. The dialog was so valuable that this became standard operating procedure across the country. Yet, another described an innovative small and medium-sized business (SMB) coverage process that rotated accounts between telecoverage and the field, allowing each mode to take the lead over a 12-month period. Result: massive uptick in SMB penetration as each channel attempted to maximize sales within a limited time window.

Last, executives spoke with passion about the importance of recognizing the efforts of sellers to contribute to the growth and success of the business. More on that in the next section.

Sellers Step It Up

Most participants in the Summits agreed that sellers are at their best when their leaders "sign them up for a mission." Participating executives noted that their best sellers are passionate about achieving goals and about being part of a growing, successful enterprise. Thus, the role of the leader in describing the mission, establishing the objectives and enlisting the support of their sellers is critical.

Yes, money is important. In the words of one participant, money is "necessary, but not sufficient." She went on to indicate that pay has to be competitive. You cannot ask top performers to work for below-market wages. But if the pay is good, then other forms of recognition are what separate the top organizations from the rest. What kind of recognition are they referring to? Here is what participating executives reported they were doing:

- One executive running a worldwide organization makes it a point to have dinner with top performers every time he is in the region…and he is in a region every week.
- One leader does a weekly video, which is broadcast to sellers every Monday morning. She reinforces the strategy, reports on progress to date and delivers shout-outs recognizing specific individuals and their accomplishments.
- Another conducts regular podcasts from every continent in which the company does business, offering news on progress to date and insight into exploits of top sellers in that particular region. You can easily believe that more than 90 percent of the sellers tune in for these podcasts (either live or recorded).
- One executive indicated that, in the face of pay freezes in 2009 he is running not one but two recognition events that year to increase the number of individuals he can publicly praise. "You cannot easily place value on this type of recognition. Let's just say it is high…very high."

What these executives share is the belief that objectives described clearly, and progress recognized publicly, are keys to enlisting the support and energy of sellers who are professionally driven to achieve goals. Said one executive, "Recognition has five times the impact of cash compensation...and delivering it is usually a matter of will, not money." The Alexander Group could not agree more.

Closing Comments

In a slow growth economy where companies are expecting revenue gains, it is no mystery why all eyes are turning to the sales organization. Now is the time for sales executives and their teams to shine. The old way of doing things will not deliver growth in this newly competitive environment. Customers are themselves expected to deliver more for less and are looking for partners to help them accomplish this feat. That will come either through price concessions or by delivering more value. Price cuts can be delivered over the Web or the phone. You don't need expensive field organizations to do that. Look for successful field sales organizations of the 21st century to earn their keep by delivering value through deep understanding of both their customers' business and their own company's capability to impact customers' top line, cost line or both. Sellers will be the linchpin to delivering value that commands premium prices and ongoing loyalty. To build such capability, look for leaders to put their energies into...

- Provisioning their sales organizations to deliver value...*think training and coaching and new alliances with marketing.*
- Enabling their sales organizations to improve organically... *think sales operations and innovation.*
- Motivating their sales organizations to deliver value to their customers and their company...*think leadership, transformation and recognition.*

Chapter 3

Better Results Through Value Selling

Author:
Gary S. Tubridy
Senior Vice President
The Alexander Group, Inc.

THE ALEXANDER GROUP'S CHIEF SALES Executive Summits in New York and Half Moon Bay, Calif., attracted 20 executives from leading firms, who discussed their views and experiences in building sales organizations that add value to the products and services they sell. It was agreed up front that value selling is an important part of most growth strategies and that the sales function is an increasingly important means of achieving competitive differentiation.

The question addressed at these sessions: *How are companies pivoting sales resources from selling things to delivering value?*

This article summarizes key points from these two Summits based on the wisdom of the attending executives regarding how companies can hone their abilities in value selling and achieve better results.

Take a New Look Around

Value is in the eyes of the customer. The key is to clarify what customers either would value (if it were available) or do value (but may not be getting). Achieving this clarification requires new and innovative processes, such as:

- *Building new functions.* New roles such as strategic insights and technology architects are emerging. Their mission: Find out what customers value, and work with product development, marketing and sales to design and distribute new offerings that serve customers better.
- *Better alignment with marketing.* Organizations are deploying marketing resources to the front line to work with both sales and customers. These field marketing teams help develop a deeper understanding of what is valued and how to deliver it using the current array of products and services.
- *Co-innovation with customers.* Important and forward-thinking customers are invited to share their insight and experience with product development teams. This increasingly common practice is shaping future products and services that have broad appeal to value-seeking customers.

The point is that the sales function cannot "dream up" good value propositions on its own. Value identification is a team sport, with the customer in a key position. New processes and new functions may help accurately identify what customers really value.

Make Some Investment

Ideas on value need to be turned into action. This requires investing in talent with deep understanding of both customer issues and the solutions you can offer. Several types of talent investments enable sellers to deliver greater value:

- *Industry principals.* Sales executives with deep experience in a given industry who can lend their expertise to solve issues with high-level counterparts on the customer side.
- *Value engineers.* Financially savvy experts who can help customers build bulletproof ROI arguments using their business model and their terminology.
- *Solution specialists.* Individuals with deep process knowledge who can assess issues and innovatively configure products and services to improve effectiveness, efficiency or both.
- *Executive account assignments.* Functional executives in sales, marketing and finance are assigned responsibility to help account managers forge high-level relationships and deliver value propositions with the gravitas that sellers alone cannot muster.

Effective value selling requires sellers to recalibrate whom they call on and how they price. Put simply, they need to call higher and price bolder.

If sellers are to succeed in this mission, they will need help… from a team with deep experience in industry issues, economics, terminology and solutions. One of the Summit attendees said, "That means our specialists are more than just a warmed-over former seller with a new title." To further realize the return on these talent investments, training and coaching for the sales teams on how to utilize these new assets is absolutely necessary.

Tell Some Stories

Stories that describe *how* your products and services have helped customers improve their businesses are a must. These can be in the form of references, cases or simply anecdotes designed to help sellers certify that they can actually deliver the value and ROI they promise. One executive referred to this as "evidence-based selling." Another comment was, "You can't expect customer attitudes or behaviors to change simply by 'challenging' them. You need evidence that you can make an impact, make a difference." Following are some suggestions on how to do this:

- *Build.* One executive expressed that "you need a process, a 'machine' to produce cases regularly." To build this machine, two things are needed:
  - Satisfied customers; the raw material that only sales can supply.
  - Customer stories; the narrative that is teased out of customers by field marketing and packaged into both cases and references.
- *Distribute.* These stories are only valuable when they make it into the hands of sellers and customers:
  - Your website should have sections devoted to the stories of successful and satisfied customers.
  - A field marketing intranet can give sellers easy access to the entire case/reference library, the latest materials and insider knowledge about how best to use the materials.
  - "Centers of excellence" have been built at some companies to showcase their latest solutions/technology, educate customer executives and facilitate introductions between high-level customer and vendor executives.
- *Refresh.* When it comes to sharing customer successes, never be satisfied, never think you are done. Always search for the latest success story to learn from and leverage. In the words of one executive, "Don't let your reference library become a museum dedicated to past success."

Hold Your Course

It takes time to build interest among the executives who matter in a value-based sale, but the payoff can be well worth the effort. You may need to build relationships with P&L level executives who are not traditionally involved in the sales process. In value selling, efficiency is not the main event. Finding ways to imbed more value in the customer contact continuum is the key. The following points can increase effectiveness:

- *Consider adding resources to lead development.* There is no waiting for the RFP in value selling. Interaction with the right customer executives can discover opportunities early, before an RFP is even contemplated. Pair account managers with inside sales resources whose job is to uncover opportunities and needs before they are expressed by the client.
- *Do not rush discovery once the lead is surfaced.* Get the facts right and build the case for action right up front. Call in the experts only if needed. Build discovery protocols to help establish the criteria for when specialist resources are needed.
- *Build the solution configuration with care.* Think of the discovery process as extended qualification. If you uncover real opportunity, then call on the resources needed to build or customize the solution that will provide customer value and win the business.
- *Selling never stops.* Ongoing service is the key to future success (and future success stories). Go-to-market leaders are taking great care to introduce a selling valence to the service role. As one executive said, "Good service today brings sales opportunities tomorrow."

Bring the Whole Team

Value selling is the opposite of "sell and run." It is what some execu-tives refer to as accountability selling, where companies invest energy across the entire customer contact continuum, from discovery to implementation and roll out. That means finding ways to work smoothly across multiple functions. Product development, marketing, sales and service need what one executive called "a shared purpose: customer success." This implies cross-functional interlock in areas such as planning, coverage, organization, job design, metrics and compensation.

But product development, marketing, sales and service have traditionally been separate or siloed. These walls need to come down or be bridged if sellers are to become partners with customer commerce leaders. One executive referred to this as developing a co-dependency between these functions. Several actions can create this co-dependency:

- *New processes.* One leader pointed to a new process that teamed up marketing and sales to produce actionable insight from customer Net Promoter scores. Marketing was tasked with identifying what specific customers loved and hated. Sales management was then charged with rapidly changing or eliminating sources of friction and scaling the practices that were deemed to be valuable.

- *New outlooks.* Good cross-functional implementation will satisfy customers and keep the door open for new sales opportunities. The viewpoint was expressed that while you don't want to turn your service organization into sellers, you do want them to be a part of the sales discussion. Service engineers need to think about selling. Field marketers need to think about customers. Sellers need to think about customer loyalty and satisfaction after the sale. A shared opinion was,

"These functions are teammates and need to understand that they do not operate alone, but are all in it together."

- *New leadership structures.* Sometimes you just need a new organization chart. To break down siloes, one Summit participant has merged sales and customer support into one group reporting to a single executive. While the organizations remain separate, common planning and metrics along with coordinated processes keep these two groups aligned. Customer support keeps a sharp eye out for opportunity while sales promotes the full spectrum of products and services, from discovery to implementation, in a more powerful voice. New leadership drives new outlooks.

Manage the Risk

Customers who buy based on value do so because they see opportunity for ROI enhancement. That usually happens by changing processes to manage costs, enhance capability or both. But in doing so, this same customer is likely exposed to new risk. Suppose the process change does not work? Suppose it is slow to produce results? Value-centric vendors need to find ways to help the customer manage these implied risks. One executive expressed, "Customers are looking for vendors to share in losses and gains, risks and benefits. They are looking for shared commitment to success." Several approaches to support this philosophy are possible:

- *Evidence.* Vendors need to make customers comfortable by pointing out where this approach has worked before. They must be prepared to connect customers with references who will share the story from an unbiased customer perspective.
- *Education.* Vendors need to provide customers with the skills and knowledge needed to leverage their newly installed purchases. This often means investment in pre- and post-sale training.

- *Terms.* Innovative terms can calibrate pricing to be more consistent with return on customer investments. Said one executive, "We are using a more strategic pricing approach to gradually align our pursuit of business with customer needs." This sometimes translates into more attractive pricing for the customer up front when they are investing in new hardware, software and processes. Over time, prices are allowed to scale up as new processes take hold and begin to deliver the promised results.

Think Like a Customer

Value selling is not for every organization. It takes time and investment to do right. Results may not be immediate. Product offerings must have sufficient breadth and complexity to create a compelling value proposition. And creating cross-functional teams can require new organization structure, processes and behaviors. Value selling is hard work.

But as one Summit attendee noted, "Value selling requires you to think like a customer. When you do this, you see the world very differently. And that can open up a whole new world of possibilities."

In an age when value means competitive advantage, companies seeking growth through sales need to think carefully about how to develop their own version of *value selling.*

SECTION II

Customer-Motivated Selling

Customer-Motivated Selling

SELLERS CAN BE EITHER motivated to sell product first or to meet customer needs first and pull products along as a result. Putting customers first is what customer-motivated selling is all about. For example, the copier salesperson stops pushing the latest model and starts looking for ways to help the client copy less, consume less paper, use less energy and recycle more. The salesperson helps the client save on costs while positioning to take a greater share of the client's copier spend. Or, the software seller stops pushing new licenses and starts working with clients to ensure proper usage of current licenses, improving client results while increasing their appetite for more licenses. Selling this way requires a new way of thinking, a new culture, new processes and programs. To get customer motivated, many sales organizations need to hit the reset button.

ARTICLES IN THIS SECTION

- Advancing the Art of Customer-Motivated Selling
- How Acting in the Customer's Best Interests Adds Growth to the Sales Equation
- Bold Moves Drive Sales Growth

Chapter 4

Advancing the Art of Customer-Motivated Selling

Author:
Gary S. Tubridy
Senior Vice President
The Alexander Group, Inc.

THE ALEXANDER GROUP CONDUCTED a series of Chief Sales Executive (CSE) Regional Forums to learn how leading-edge companies are succeeding in their effort to win through the added value of customer-motivated selling. These events featured keynote speakers who represent companies that have launched customer-motivated selling initiatives that include elements of solution selling, trusted advisor relationships and a measure of mutual self-interest.

This executive summary captures the insights and ideas expressed at the 2010 Regional Forums by both keynote speakers and participants on how to defeat the commodity trap and improve differentiation by implementing a customer-motivated selling strategy.

What Is Customer-Motivated Selling?

Sales executives agree. Post-recession buyers are more informed and more demanding. Sellers are hearing "I want more discounts, I want more service and if I don't get it there are options!" Sales executives are actively seeking ways to avoid this commodity trap. Many are asking their sellers to add value by helping customers to use the products and services they carry to improve business processes and deliver real ROI. Customer-motivated selling depends on tuning products and services to meet the customer's business needs and deploying sales resources who can deliver economic value to customer and supplier alike.

Why Consider Customer-Motivated Selling?

Not all companies need to add value to their products. For those with "killer products" (i.e., short supply and high demand), selling means taking orders. The last thing they want is to add value and lengthen the sales cycle…there are orders to take!

If the product line is simple (food products for instance) or well understood (automobiles), then the seller's ability to add value by infusing knowledge or problem solving competence is limited. Alternate channels that maximize efficiency over effectiveness are often preferable.

But for many companies with broad product lines, it's not that simple. They have products spanning the entire customer engagement life cycle, some simple, and some complex. Taken as a whole, particularly among larger Fortune 1000 companies, such product lines often warrant the attention of sellers who bring application expertise to the table and who can design multi-product configurations.

Here's where customer-motivated selling turns the traditional sales equation around. Instead of pumping customer contacts for their product needs, these sellers search for opportunities to solve their customers' most vexing problems. The copier salesperson stops pushing the latest model and starts looking for ways to help the client copy less, consume less paper, use less energy and recycle more. He/she helps the client save on costs while positioning to take a greater share of the client's copier spend. Or, the software seller stops pushing new licenses and starts working with clients to ensure proper usage of current licenses, improving client results while increasing their appetite for more licenses.

Forum participants recognize that many customers will pay a premium for solutions to their business problems. They know that these customers, like them, face an economic climate in which they must deliver more with less. But they are not naïve. They know that delivering value comes neither fast nor cheap. Which begs the question: "Is customer-motivated selling worth it?" Here is what our speakers and guests had to say on what customer-motivated selling has meant to them:

Higher returns. As one speaker reported, "Our studies indicate that we get a 3.9 percent return on investment in capital items vs. an 8.5 percent return on investment in human capital. Producing a more knowledgeable sales force has been an excellent investment for us." What drives this finding? "Sellers who are knowledge workers help command higher prices and deeper customer loyalty. The competition can't easily match that." Building on this point, another speaker added, "We won't get our target return on investment if the money put into new product development isn't complemented with investment in the resources needed to sell them."

Faster growth. Multiple speakers cited evidence of faster growth in segments where they positioned themselves as solution partners. One executive pointed to 30 percent share gains in segments targeted with partnering strategies vs. other segments where they suffered a 20 percent share loss. Another speaker who placed a big bet on transformation to solution selling in 2009 cited growth exceeding 5 percent while "competitors were scratching just to stay flat." As far as he was concerned, solution selling was the "right bet."

Greater differentiation. In a competitive world where products can look pretty similar, your sales organization's ability to deliver value beyond the product feature envelope can be a meaningful and sustainable way to differentiate. Said one guest, "Competitors can copy our products, but they can't easily imitate the value we deliver through our sellers. Value through people is something you have to build from the ground up; there are no shortcuts."

Market insight. Customer-motivated sales organizations stay closer to their customers and get more insight into what they value. For example, an executive from the medical products industry described how client insight from sellers led to a new and highly differentiated product. "Cardiothoracic surgeons complained about patient trauma caused by surgical procedures requiring removal of ribs to access the chest cavity. Sellers asked, 'Can you develop an instrument that goes in between the ribs so doctors won't have to take them out?'" This insight resulted in development of a minimally invasive instrument, now a client favorite. Market insight, driven by proximity to the customer and a willingness to listen, led the way to sustainable profit.

Where to Add Value

While a customer-motivated approach that adds value through sellers is certainly worth considering, not all customers care to partner with suppliers. Nor can suppliers afford to provide the same level of partnership to all customers large and small. So, how does the customer-motivated sales organization decide where and what value to add? Here is how one speaker thought about it: "Buyers come in three flavors:

1. *Price conscious*…product features matter, but the best price likely wins the business.
2. *Relationship-minded*…relationship matters, but that gets you right of refusal. You need to meet the price of the low-cost supplier.

3. *Partner-oriented*…for these customers, ideas matter. They award their business to partners who show them how to improve business processes and get better results.

"You need to determine where each customer falls and to give them the kind of coverage that meets their needs." Implicit in this statement is the fact that labor-intensive value selling will only deliver a reasonable return among partner-oriented customers.

Building on that, another speaker noted that the coverage you can afford generally corresponds with the size of the account you are targeting. Consider the following coverage model and value propositions:

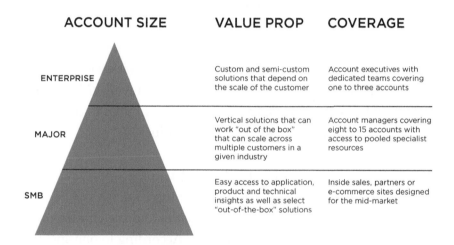

ACCOUNT SIZE	VALUE PROP	COVERAGE
ENTERPRISE	Custom and semi-custom solutions that depend on the scale of the customer	Account executives with dedicated teams covering one to three accounts
MAJOR	Vertical solutions that can work "out of the box" that can scale across multiple customers in a given industry	Account managers covering eight to 15 accounts with access to pooled specialist resources
SMB	Easy access to application, product and technical insights as well as select "out-of-the-box" solutions	Inside sales, partners or e-commerce sites designed for the mid-market

Said this executive about the keys to making this model work:

1. "Clarify the value customers can expect from you." At the enterprise level of account, you can afford to do some customization. Below that level, you need to develop more scalable out-of-the box solutions.
2. "Organize to deliver that value as efficiently as possible." Be innovative about how you deploy specialists at the major account level. Use technology (video, Web, etc.) to

efficiently deliver expertise. Develop clear rules on how and when to involve specialists to avoid waste.

Key point: Success in customer-motivated selling means understanding what customers value and delivering it as efficiently as possible. One executive summed it up nicely: "The best value-added selling strategy begins with comprehensive account segmentation. Success means giving customers what they *need*, not simply what you want to *sell*."

How to Add Value

According to one executive, sellers add value by using "fundamental knowledge of their customers' business processes to suggest ways that their products and services can improve efficiency, effectiveness or both." However, as another speaker stated, "that is easier said than done." What is needed to make this objective a reality? Following are the six levers that our speakers felt were essential to translate a customer-motivated strategy into sales results.

1. *Top management commitment.* Customer-motivated selling must be fully embraced by top leadership. CSE support alone is insufficient to withstand the challenges of value-selling implementation. According to one speaker, customer-motivated selling "does not generally bear fruit in the first quarter you try it. You have to stick with it." The C-suite and the top sales executive need a shared investment appetite, ROI timeline and sense of destiny.

2. *Sales executive commitment.* Results from value selling don't accrue overnight. It takes time to achieve momentum. The top sales executive and his or her team need to demonstrate commitment to customer-motivated selling, especially if pressure mounts among veterans to "go back to the old

way" in the interests of generating quick results. Such backsliding signals to the sales force that a value-centric sales strategy is simply the "flavor of the month" and will disappear if "you can just outlast it."

3. *Marketing commitment.* Traditional marketing support characterized by the handoff of cold leads and product-centric promotion materials needs significant updating. As one speaker noted, "Marketing has to work in parallel with sales, not in sequence." Meaning that marketing needs to offer support consistent with a longer and somewhat more complex sales process, including:

- Elevating the brand image in selected solutions/ verticals.
- Packaging solution offerings and associated materials for sellers to use.
- Supplying or funding expertise and training in relevant solutions/industries.
- Collecting seller input on successes and failures both to learn and to identify strong references.

Marketing and sales interact and support each other every step of the way to ensure maximum effectiveness in a more complex selling environment.

4. *Investment.* Investment in tactical support is needed in three areas to help sellers succeed at customer-motivated selling:

Wisdom. Sellers need to know the special issues associated with their customers' business. As one speaker reported, "Sellers need to fully understand and use the vocabulary of their customers." As well, they need to grasp the culture/ decision-making process of their customers to better know how and when to position their solutions. This requires core training in vertical business issues and executive selling.

Technical expertise. Even with proper training, sellers cannot know everything. As one speaker said, "Sellers can at best acquire T-shaped knowledge," enabling them to represent their service line broadly enough to spot opportunities but able to go deep in only one or two solutions. Where seller knowledge is shallow, supplemental expertise is required in the form of solution/product experts, vertical experts or both. It is not enough for sellers to be generalists who depend on specialists to "weave products into solutions," said one speaker. Sellers must themselves have the capability to spot and qualify selected solution opportunities to earn a place at the customer planning table. Availability of technical expertise complements wisdom...it does not replace it.

Time. No account exploration, no specialist collaboration, no executive relationships happen if sellers don't manage their time differently and better. Two aspects of time management are most frequently in need of modification: account targeting and post-sale service. As one speaker reported, "Account lists for our sellers used to be long. We now ask our sellers to go deep in only five accounts or less, instead of tree topping 20 or 30. We clarified where we wanted them to focus." Post-sale service can also be a time sink. From order processing to problem resolution, companies need to invest in lower cost people and/or systems to relieve the account manager of routine activities and enable them to focus more time on finding and selling solutions.

5. *People.* The right skill and experience mix among sellers and specialists is vital to delivering value in a customer-motivated culture. Speakers and guests noted four areas where they are resolved to upping their game:

Talent. Many companies now seek sellers with vertical experience, knowing it is easier to imbed product and solution knowledge than it is to transfer vertical expertise.

Assessment. Some executives estimate that fewer than half of their current sellers are capable of succeeding in a solution selling world. They are gearing up to assess solution selling ability and recruit new talent to fill gaps. Said one executive, "This is no time to be sentimental."

Training. Most executives indicate that training budgets remained fully funded in 2010. Several anticipate increased funding in 2011. Training objectives are decidedly tilted toward business process/solution design and executive selling skills.

Coaching. Front-line managers are critical to the transformation to value selling. Most companies are working hard at giving these managers the necessary coaching skills (sometimes referred to as "coaching boot camp") and increasing the amount of time they devote to coaching (from an average of less than 7 percent to more than 20 percent). As one speaker pointed out, "The key to transforming to a solution sales model is getting the line mangers engaged in it." Implied point: Coaches must also experience elements of solution selling/executive sales training to be better coaches for their sellers.

6. *Execution.* The best way to execute complex solution selling is to "make it easy" as well as to "make it worth their while." To this end, many of our speakers are turning to playbooks that provide a common source for all contributors to the sales process to draw upon for:

- High-impact value propositions.

- Power messages for use at various points along the sales continuum.
- Qualification guidelines.
- Sales process steps and guidelines for who is responsible for various activities/results in a complex sales process.

Several executives admitted that modifying measurement and compensation practices was necessary to mitigate the risk for sellers in undertaking more complex sales processes. For instance, as sales processes elongate, some money at risk is being shifted into base salary or into bonuses based on achieving sales process milestones or product/service mix goals.

Advice

What did speakers learn from their efforts that they would pass along to their peers? Consider the following pointers:

1. *Focus.* Only try to add value where you have a reasonable chance of success based on your current products, current customers and current domain expertise. You can't make value appear out of thin air.
2. *Scalability.* Make sure the solutions and value propositions you develop are attractive to whole segments, not just one customer. It takes a lot of time and effort to create and deliver a solution; volume and profitability depend on scale. Solutions in verticals where you are already a player are a good place to start.
3. *Clear rules of engagement.* In a complex sales process, make sure all stakeholders (sellers, specialists, partners, customer resources) know what to expect and when.
4. *Customer churn.* Constantly review customer churn to learn why customers leave; spot emerging trends and

opportunities and be prepared to move fast. No snoozing means no losing.

5. *Pipeline management.* Longer more complex sales processes can lead to dry spells if sales opportunities are not properly managed and timed. Use your CRM system to help manage this potential choke point.

6. *Consider a "horizontal skunk works" to get initial traction.* Bring product development, marketing and sales together in an informal "skunk works" to get a vertical or a particular solution up and running quickly. These are the functions that can rapidly create the messages, deliverables, tools and capabilities needed to succeed out of the box. And in the event of a slow start, it helps to have friends.

7. *Building a customer-motivated sales force* to deliver real solutions is no silver bullet. It takes time, effort and investment. This is a good news/bad news story. Customer-motivated selling isn't easy…that's the bad news. But if you get it right, chances are you will end up way ahead of your competitors—precisely because it is so tough. That's the good news.

8. *If you are an ambitious sales executive* looking to put distance between you and the competition, solution selling in a customer-motivated culture is an option you need to explore.

Chapter 5

How Acting in the Customer's Best Interests Adds Growth to the Sales Equation

Author:
Gary S. Tubridy
Senior Vice President
The Alexander Group, Inc.

THE ALEXANDER GROUP'S Chief Sales Executive (CSE) Forum attracts speakers from some of the finest organizations in the world. This article describes in more detail what was learned from the CSE Forum speakers and the survey respondents about what they are doing to build and leverage customer-motivated sales organizations to support their strategic growth plans.

What is a customer-motivated organization? Customer-motivated sales organizations understand the pressures their customers are under. They use this understanding to differentiate themselves from the competition by discovering what their customers truly value and aligning their sales teams to provide it. They package and position their products and services to help their customers achieve goals and overcome obstacles.

Good News, Bad News

The main message from the *2010/2011 Sales Pulse Survey* is very clear...growth is back on the table for 2011 and beyond. Consider these statistics:

- 64 percent of respondents report 2010 attainment is above plan.
- 82 percent of respondents predict that in 2011 the company will perform better than 2010.
- More than half see some growth in the economy in 2011.
- 68 percent plan to increase their investment in the sales force in 2011.

Not far beneath these rosy numbers, however, is a starker reality:

- In 2010, the average growth expectation is 6 percent.
- While most organizations will increase their investment in sales resources in 2011, sales assets will, on average, increase only 1.5 percent.

This is the 2011 paradox: Grow sales rapidly, but grow sales resources slowly.

Leading companies will step up to the challenge of meeting these aggressive objectives by adopting a customer-motivated philosophy. They believe that by integrating sales' intellectual capital and expertise into products and services they create meaningful differentiation from the competition, enabling:

- Better pricing and margins.
- Stronger relationships with higher level executives.
- More frequent wins with more valuable solutions.

In short, they plan to win by building *customer-motivated* sales organizations.

Building A Customer-Motivated Sales Culture

CSE Forum speakers were clear about what is needed to build a customer-motivated sales organization.

1. *Give the sales force a customer-motivated mission.* As Jill Brannon of FedEx stated, you "sell from the outside in; customer needs dictate how you organize sales resources." Mike Fasulo of Sony described a culture that "derives from the customer and the consumer." Some speakers took that a step further. Neil Isford of IBM referenced the need for a company to engage the sales force in representing an enduring idea. In the case of a product-oriented company, the enduring idea revolves around the product...such as BMW and the enduring idea of "exhilaration." However, for companies in the B2B world, a customer-motivated mission is more complex. Buyers are looking less at product and more at outcomes. The experience of the customer does not revolve around a brand as much as the entire sales interaction. As Isford stated, the enduring value of doing business with IBM is "experienced through the IBM sales team." In a world where lots of products are functionally equivalent (or close enough), it is *the seller* who makes the difference. Smart companies must acknowledge this and assertively position the seller directly in the middle of the value proposition. The customer-motivated mission of sellers is to make themselves indispensable to the customer.

2. *Leverage the full value of sales intellectual property.* In a culture built on customer motivation, it is recognized that the sales organization holds insight into how to deliver value to customers and develop lasting relationships. These companies

know that products and services do not stand alone; that adept sellers position, package and deliver combinations of product and service designed to meet customer needs and solve problems. How is this done?

Specialization. Whether it means investing in verticals, engaging partners with deep, relevant experience or finding ways to use telesales to deliver more expertise at less cost, speakers were clear on the need to imbed expertise that customers value in the sales process.

Leadership engagement. The very highest levels in a customer-motivated organization are engaged in customer interaction to both reach customer executives and to personally observe what sellers do to deliver value. Customers value it. Sellers appreciate it. Executives see first-hand what a customer-motivated culture can accomplish.

Tools. The right tools give sellers greater productivity and easier access to knowledge. FedEx uses social networking technology to link sellers with peers who offer the latest insights. Cisco has built a Sales Acceleration Center to provide needed expertise 24/7…anytime, anywhere.

Long view. Customer-motivated organizations are focused as much on the customer experience as they are on near-term results. As customers increasingly seek better outcomes, these companies make the investments needed to create closer, partner-level relationships with their customers. As one executive said, his sellers "provoke the conversation, engage in the issues, convene the experts and propose a solution." Expertise and dedication to service are imbedded in a process designed to deliver customer value.

3. *Innovate and operationalize.* Reported Bill LePage of Cisco, "You need to balance innovation with operational excellence."

Business complexity is going up, but sellers and sales leaders want selling complexity to go down. You cannot solve problems for customers when you are busy creating problems for yourself. Customer-motivated sales organizations have a willingness to create value for customers with new solutions and specialists, along with detailed rules of engagement that create understanding about who does what, when. Examples abound:

FedEx uses social networking to share best practices among its sellers. Cisco is leading the charge toward virtualizing support resources with centers of excellence connected to the field with technology such as telepresence and shared databases of vital information, which are open to all sellers, all the time.

Honeywell is innovating with incentives such as the Circle of Excellence program, allowing sellers who surpass a performance threshold to attend an award event…and invite a member of their team who was instrumental to their success. Or, the Hero Award Program which lets sellers share a portion of their incentive pay (typically in the 10 percent to 30 percent range) with key support staff who helped them deliver value.

These companies combine a bias toward innovation (and a willingness to try new things) with a mandate for operational efficiency. What emerges are new ideas and systems that enable sales excellence and foster a customer-motivated attitude.

4. *Lead from the front.* There is no substitute for leaders who demonstrate their commitment to building a sales organization capable of separating from the pack, of being what one executive referred to as "the winning difference in

the competitive showdown." Isford of IBM refers to this as a "personal commitment not just to sell and tell, but to learn," which is demonstrated by visibility in the field and by making tangible changes to resolve real, day-to-day issues. These sales executives take care to communicate what they have learned and what they are doing to make things better. Isford communicates to his organization through blogs and podcasts. Reported LePage of Cisco, the main job of the top sales executive is to "communicate, communicate, then communicate some more." Cisco executives have a mission to "create a common, compelling vision in which everyone is all in." That means being out there, "doing the right thing" and giving the organization good reasons to follow you. LePage continued, "In doing this, you have to realize this is a marathon, not a sprint." For executives who want sales excellence and want their sellers to be the winning difference, persistence in personally leading them toward a truly customer-motivated culture cannot be overstated.

Building Blocks

What are companies doing to support implementation of a customer-motivated sales philosophy? According to the *2010/2011 Sales Pulse Survey*, expected changes in headcount this year will be modest across the organization. Field sales, inside sales and sales operations will only add an average of 0.1 percent to 1.9 percent sales headcount.

Executives at Fortune 1000 companies are on the whole not planning to grow selling resources of any type nearly as fast as they expect to grow sales (6 percent median growth rate). This does not mean they are not spending judiciously…they are. Instead of pouring money into resources to run the same old play, many executives are rewriting the playbook. As noted above, the keynote speakers at the 2010 Forum are investing to position their sales forces to deliver value and differentiate from the competition. The *Sales Pulse Survey* also asked respondents for insight into their sales investment strategy and, in particular, how their sales resources will add value. Here are the top answers:

What is the most important way in which sellers will add value in 2011?	38% said...	Sellers will deliver better solutions to their customers' most pressing business needs.
	26% said...	Sellers will demonstrably link the products and services they deliver to ROI for their customers.

What single initiative will have the most impact on results in 2011?	30% said...	Redefine the coverage model to increase expertise in accounts that are the highest growth prospects.
	26% said...	Redefine the sales process to deliver more value to customers.

   Bottom line: These companies are putting in place the building blocks of a customer-motivated sales culture by judiciously investing in programs to help their sellers deliver measurable value.

Delivering Solutions with ROI to the Customer

The philosophy of bringing important and measurable value to customers is at the heart of customer-motivated selling. The gutsy leadership needed to invest in innovation that leverages sales IP is on full display among the executives participating in this survey. Said one, "We need to be out in front offering our customers thought leadership. Success means bringing solutions that benefit the owners of important problems." As another executive indicated, this means "being a source of information on new and better ways of doing business." These executives want their sellers to be valued for their wisdom and experience, for their "depth of subject matter expertise" above and beyond the benefits generally associated with their product portfolios.

For these executives, execution is as important as ideas in the value equation. Ideas get you to the discussion. Implemented solutions get you invited back. These executives want to help their customers "make more money." They want to "deliver on cost savings, productivity improvements and top-line growth." They cited several ways to get sellers engaged in the ROI discussion, including:

1. Prepare sellers for "much deeper discovery to ensure the root issues are found."
2. Invest in sellers with "deep vertical expertise," who understand "unique vertical business drivers."
3. Describe customer issues using "customer language; show them you understand."
4. Show how a solution will affect the top line; "help our customers sell more by giving them access to better information" and "providing education to help them make best use of this new information."
5. Show how a solution will affect operations by using specific examples such as "helping reduce customer churn" or "producing invoices more efficiently."

6. Show how a solution minimizes cost by "taking cost out of inventory" or "reducing the total cost of operations" by increasing productivity and allowing the customer to do more with less.

Ideally, they will do all of this by enabling their sellers to utilize the full breadth of their products and services in a unique combination that is difficult if not outright impossible for the competition to emulate.

Investing in Initiatives that Matter

As previously referenced, 30 percent of participants in the *Sales Pulse Survey* tell us the single most important initiative they are investing in is transforming the coverage model to inject more value into the sales equation. Another 26 percent say the most important initiative on their agenda is re-engineering the sales process to deliver more value to customers.

Both concepts are right. These investments mirror the ambitions of the CSE Forum keynote speakers who believe that sales effort and expertise set their companies apart and are central to achieving growth ambitions in an intensely competitive market. The initiatives they are investing in to enhance the value their sellers deliver fall into two categories:

1. Initiatives to inject greater value into the sales equation by transforming the coverage model (how sellers access, persuade and fulfill obligations to customers) are being launched across industries from high-tech software to medical devices:

ACCESS	PERSUADE	FULFILL
Focus on C-level execs with broader vision and responsibility.	Invest in sales ops to deliver 24/7 support to seller before, during and after the sale.	Invest in sales support engineers to offload critical implementation responsibilities, thus freeing up time for account penetration.
Use technology to deliver greater insight at the point of contact on industry issues and potential solutions (such as the iPad).	Invest in building centers of excellence and telepresence technology to give sellers access to discovery, technical and solution development support 24/7 globally.	
	Insert strong qualification standards into initial stages of the sale to "lose early," before investing resources in an already lost cause.	

2. Investments to inject value into the coverage model are being made across all types of customer accounts:

INVESTMENTS	ACCOUNT TYPE		
	GLOBAL	NATIONAL	LOCAL
Introduce inside sales coverage		•	•
Increase the number of vertical/technical specialists	•	•	
Select channel partners based on expertise not volume	•	•	•
Virtual support centers with 24/7 access to technical expertise	•	•	•

It is important to note that these investments are often not wholly incremental. For instance, as more resource is shifted into specialists, resources in other sectors are diminished. This resource shift accounts for the rising prominence of inside sales in some forward-thinking companies as a means to reach more customers with a value message, in a very efficient way.

Embracing Change in the Name of Customer Motivation

Customer motivation depends on a willingness to try new things, see what works, scale the winning ideas and scrap the losers. It calls for both agility and adaptability and recognition that what works today cannot be presumed to work tomorrow. Customer motivation calls for curiosity about uncovering and leveraging the next great opportunity to add lasting value through sales excellence. To paraphrase LePage of Cisco, this means:

- Use the insight of the sales force to ascertain where customers are going and how the sales team must in turn prepare to support this journey. Design the future from the future.
- Be prepared to confront reality…know when and where change is needed and do not allow inertia to stand in the way.
- Create a common and compelling vision for the sales team about why change is needed and what is in it for the team as a whole and for them as individuals.
- Assess the situation and then reassess. Never assume that the process or the outcomes are a given.
- Be principled, yet adaptable. Be willing to change the process in the interest of achieving the long-term objective.
- Communicate, communicate and then communicate some more.

Closing Comments

An Alexander Group client recently said, "You know you have a customer-motivated sales force when the customer will almost pay you to sell to them. Instead of chasing demand, you are introducing new concepts, demonstrating new value and creating new demand." That is how customer-motivated sales organizations both support their core business and find future growth opportunities.

Increasingly, sales organizations are responsible for identifying customer needs, and then crafting and delivering solutions to meet those needs. They are expected to be an equal partner with marketing and product development in this mission. This is only possible by adopting the ideas and initiatives shown by leading companies that embrace a customer-motivated culture. Companies that are stuck in tactical execution divorced from a strategic mission need to consider radical changes to their sales model. Transforming to a customer-motivated sales organization may well prove to be the best strategy for sustainable growth in 2011 and beyond.

Chapter 6

Bold Moves Drive Sales Growth

Author:
Gary S. Tubridy
Senior Vice President
The Alexander Group, Inc.

THE ALEXANDER GROUP (AGI) explored the bold moves that leading companies made to secure their growth ambitions through expertise and intellectual capital delivered by their sales organizations. One word binds all these moves together...value.

Sales organizations have the ability to add value to the products and services they sell. Top executives know that adding value through sales builds differentiation that is hard for competitors to match. Enabling sales organizations to deliver such value in tough and competitive markets requires bold moves.

Based on insights shared by the speakers at the 2012 Regional and Annual Chief Sales Executive Forums, we have distilled 10 of these bold moves into three categories:

Go where the growth is...	1. Segment customers by what they value 2. Focus sellers where their efforts count 3. Use new channels to reach new segments
Retool sales tactics...	4. Do more with less through better analytics 5. Enrich the number of sales motions you can deliver 6. Influence up by expanding the sales process 7. Talk ROI
Get serious about implementation...	8. Signal that you mean it 9. Practice tough love 10. Inspire a value-centric culture

This executive summary details these bold moves to deliver customer value and drive sales growth.

Go Where the Growth Is

Sales organizations rarely achieve aggressive growth objectives by chasing the same old targets. Yet, year after year, most sales resources are allocated to servicing legacy accounts with little or no growth potential. Making the growth number means driving limited and expensive sales resources to where they can make a difference. Bold moves that produce better segmentation, focus and coverage can help make this happen.

1. *Segment customers by what they value.* Most segmentation groups accounts by size: global, national, regional and small and medium-sized business (SMB). More sophisticated models introduce sales potential. But in an era of intensifying cost pressure, a third dimension needs to be considered: *What do customers value?* Do they seek the lowest possible cost? Or do they seek applications and insight that will help them run their businesses more efficiently and profitably?

Segmentation models that do not account for this "value" dimension can lead to wasteful coverage decisions. Consider the huge account that simply wants the best possible price every time. They do all their business through RFPs and always take the low bid. Such accounts are little more than "RFP bullies," who demand steep discounts on the strength of their size. Such accounts deserve nothing more than the lowest cost resource it takes to submit an RFP/bid. Yet, in many cases, based on size alone, these accounts are assigned to top sellers. This is wasteful. Don't ignore these accounts, but don't get fooled by their size...you can't make it up on volume when each unit is sold at break-even or worse.

On the other hand, there are accounts that assign great value to the insight they get from vendors that show how the smart use of their products and services can provide a competitive advantage. If a vendor shows them how to save money—money that can be applied to other investments—customers are comfortable paying a premium for the combination of products and intellectual capital supplied.

2. *Focus sellers where their efforts count.* This is no small thing. AGI benchmarks show that year after year, two things are true about sellers:

- Only 40 percent of their time (at best) is devoted to actual selling.
- More than 75 percent of this time goes to maintaining *current relationships.*

It is highly likely that only a portion of current customers has both growth potential and an eye for vendors that deliver value; therefore, it is also likely that much of the available selling resource is misallocated.

Simply put, the amount of sales time devoted to finding new value-centric accounts will need to increase dramatically. Forum speakers had a few recommendations to make this happen:

- *Find value-centric accounts in the planning process.* Profile value-centric accounts in terms of products and services they typically buy, who does the buying, the basis on which buying decisions are made, price points at which they buy and industries in which they participate. Use your sales ops capability to help identify target accounts in each territory, district and region. Articulate the amount of business that you expect to come from value-centric accounts. Define the amount of time sellers should devote to them and build your expectations into metrics, goals and compensation programs.
- *Build new processes to service current accounts that you value but which have little potential for growth.* Consider building out a service function, perhaps one that is based inside. Demonstrate to sellers that old accounts will be well served while they are on the hunt for new and more profitable business.
- *Show sellers that the new approach works.* Consider starting with a trial involving several top sellers. Invest in converting these thought leaders into cheerleaders. Test and refine the new approach with their input and expertise. Use their early success stories and examples to convince the rest of the organization that they too can succeed.

3. *Use new channels to reach new segments.* New channels can help a company gain access to new segments quickly and economically. For instance, several speakers referenced the middle market as a potentially lucrative but problematic segment. This market is often underserved but willing to pay a premium for services and insight. However, there is a challenge in covering a segment composed of larger numbers of smaller accounts.

Andrew Sage, vice president of Worldwide Partner Led at Cisco Systems, described how his world is divided into three basic segments: large accounts covered by account managers; middle market accounts covered by territory managers; and SMB accounts covered by channel partners. He suggested a two-pronged strategy to improve middle-market coverage:

- Force territory managers (TM) to cover fewer, larger accounts in the middle market. This may require fewer TMs, where the remaining ones are forced to go deeper in the accounts they cover to meet their growth goals. Result: growth through insight and leveraged relationships—not cherry picking.
- Assign lower-end accounts formerly covered by TMs to channel partners. Remember, these are the accounts that were the smallest in the TM patch. As a whole, they were likely under-covered. Give these accounts to good partners and three things happen:
  - The partner is appreciative. The good ones always want more.
  - The customer is appreciative. They have never been given especially good coverage by the TM, so the attention they get from the channel partner is a big improvement.

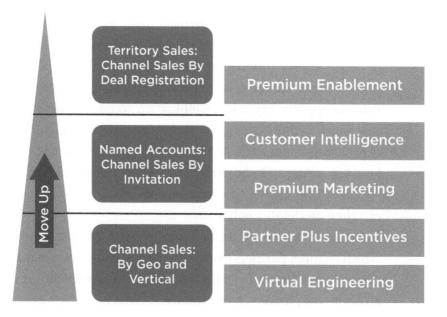

○ Penetration and results go up. More coverage at no added fixed cost is good for the bottom line.

Retool Sales Tactics

Longer, more complex sales processes in a post-recession economy mean more decision makers with different needs and expectations. Sellers need new messages, new targets and new approaches to make an impact. The best sales organizations will use such complexity to their advantage.

4. *Do more with less through better analytics.* Big data can lead to deeper insight if you improve sales analytics. Top companies are using enhanced sales analytics to improve segmentation, create better dashboards and upgrade their relationships with business partners. Often undertaken by the increasingly important sales operations department, sales analytics is the combination of data, software and management insight that produces:

- *Better customer segmentation.* Sales analytics can provide insight into which customer types are most likely to buy and when. By using what is known about highly penetrated accounts (i.e., sales history, products and services bought, buying cycle), sales analytics can be used to project the shape and potential value of opportunity at less well-known accounts. This offers the ability to more accurately target limited sales resources.
- *Better understanding of the best attributes of top sellers.* By tracking how top sellers spend their time, sales operations can create "profiles" of what they do. Other sellers (and their managers) can then model this behavior.
- *Better understanding of the best channel partners.* By tracking which channel partners close which leads, companies can do a better job of both efficiently allocating leads and identifying attributes of partners that produce success in a given area.

5. *Enrich the number of sales motions you can deliver.* If the majority of seller time is spent servicing current customers, then sellers are likely to be familiar with only one or two sales motions:

- *"Showing"* current products to customers…where discussions tend to degrade to bargaining over price and terms.
- *"Bundling"* current products into a more comprehensive package with a higher price point…and deeper discounts.

Yet, there are other sales motions that matter to a sales executive who wants his or her sales force to deliver value…motions that are often overlooked when the focus is on servicing the current sales base:

- *"Teaching"* customers about the features of new products and how they can be used to improve their way of doing business.
- *"Solution selling"* configurations of new and old products along with services that help customers solve known problems in important areas of their business.
- *"Vision selling"* using deep insight into customer business plans to demonstrate how a configuration of products and services can help the customer run the business differently and better, thus conferring some level of competitive advantage.

If profitable growth depends on delivering value, then the "show" and "bundle" sales motions are certainly not the keys to success. Sales executives need to invest in the mix of jobs, processes, training and tools to enable their sales resources to deliver on *all* these sales motions, simultaneously and well.

Deliver value to customers who seek it. Deliver products at the best possible price to customers who expect this. But cover segments differently according to need. Enriching the number of sales motions deployed allows sales executives to focus their expensive and limited resources where they can make a difference.

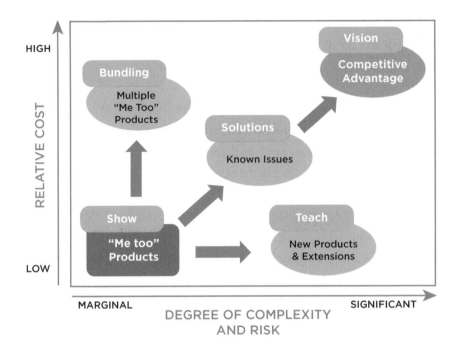

6. *Influence up by expanding the sales process.* With more influencers entering the sales process, much is said about the need to shorten the sales cycle. Forum speakers indicated this is only half right. Efficiency is laudable when showing products and emphasizing price or features. But when value is the key, an efficient sales process is the last thing you should be trying to employ.

According to our speakers, sellers need to "lean into and expand the sales process" making sure that buyers who care about value are included in decision making. This takes time. Legacy contacts in middle management and procurement have little interest in improving efficiency or enhancing revenue. General managers and functional executives do. Strategy-minded sales executives who depend on selling value know that only sales organizations willing to invest the time to build C-suite contacts will succeed in the long run. By reaching the right buyer with the right message, they know that they will win more profitable business.

Often, this means finding the opportunity before the customer does.

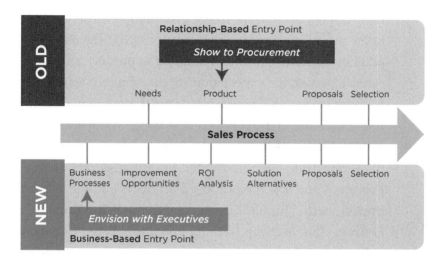

Glenn Mason, president of Global Sales Strategy and Sales Operations at UPS, estimates that almost 60 percent of the deals that come to sellers are already decided before the RFP is even issued. Spending time on such RFPs is often a waste of time and effort. The best sellers invest time upstream to uncover opportunities and either bypass the RFP process altogether or shape it in their favor. This does not shorten the sales process. It lengthens it. Sellers who expand the sales process by reaching out and finding opportunities that interest higher level executives before they even know an opportunity exists exemplify value selling.

7. *Talk ROI.* Once in the executive suite, sellers need to speak the right language. This means speaking ROI. Forum speakers admitted that while they hear lots about the need for ROI fluency, they see it only rarely. What is needed to achieve fluency in the language of ROI? Three items were pointed out:

- *Definition.* Many ROI pitches revolve around templates, which depend on "plugging in" select assumptions about cost savings, revenue uplift and product/service prices. Yet, most businesses have their own unique ways to justify spend on the basis of

ROI. Clients don't want to see your template; they want to know that sellers understand their approach to calculating ROI and have utilized this understanding to produce an estimate consistent with the expectations of their finance team.

- *Business process.* ROI assumptions need more than a cursory understanding of the very business processes that will hopefully be improved to deliver the assumed return. Sellers need to demonstrate deep understanding of customer business processes and *how* the proposed products and services will impact them. This adds legitimacy to the ROI estimates.

- *Delivery.* Talk is cheap. Talking about ROI is not as good as delivering it. Executives want to see vendors who can deliver on the ROI that is promised. Performance guarantees are good. Even more powerful is the offer of "skin in the game"… money at risk that the vendor is willing to put on the table in return for the sale.

Get Serious About Implementation

Legacy practices for sales metrics, compensation and talent development won't get you where you need to go. Delivering more value through the sales function means adding new jobs, new processes and new behaviors. If you want all that to work in harmony, take a serious approach to implementation.

8. *Signal that you mean it.* Sellers know the difference between a serious shift in strategy and the "strategy du jour." And they are watching. When the company is serious, it places the weight of new metrics, goals and compensation behind any shift in message and strategy. If you are serious about delivering value to the segments that demand it, you need to:

- Create and populate the jobs needed to deliver it (generalists and specialists).

- Create the rules of engagement needed to effectively and efficiently deploy this talent against the right opportunities.
- Attach different metrics to each job according to the outcomes expected.
- Target the right sales compensation plans to each job, placing more risk and leverage against transactional sales jobs, and less against jobs that are expected to deliver value to customers over a longer period of time.

If you want your sellers to act differently, send the right signals. Be clear about what you expect by aligning the rules, metrics and pay.

9. *Practice tough love.* Selling on the basis of value will require a change in behavior on the part of many incumbents. When such change is expected there are four possible outcomes, illustrated here:

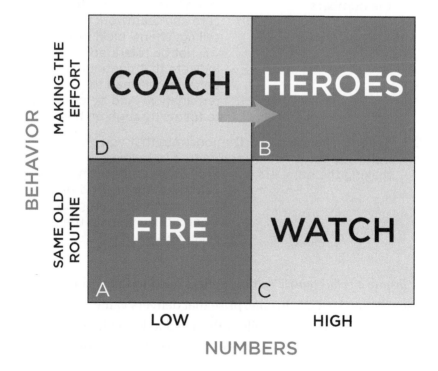

Tough love means committing to one of four possible actions to deal with these outcomes:

SITUATION		ACTION
A	Seller is neither changing behavior nor making the numbers...they run the same old plays	Terminate quickly
B	Seller is changing behavior and making the numbers... demonstrating successful adoption	Recognize quickly
C	Seller is not changing behavior but is still making the numbers	Get tough and recommunicate what is expected • Tell them that behavior inconsistent with customer care and teamwork (push selling, cherry picking, etc.) will not be tolerated • Indicate that continued behavior will lead to termination. And be prepared to follow through on this.
D	Seller is changing behavior but is not making the numbers	Demonstrate that you are committed to helping • Provide the support needed to help them turn the corner • Plan, coach, encourage...do what it takes to help them succeed

10. *Inspire a value-centric culture.* Sellers need to know they are part of something special, an enterprise that delivers value and has deep respect for the customer. Sellers also need to know that they are an integral part of this value equation. Mason of UPS commented, "You

need to go broader and deeper in accounts. You have to find the opportunities before the customer finds them. You've got to engage early in the sales process to shape opportunities. When you do, you demonstrate a keen understanding of their business and all of the relevant alternatives."

Value-centric cultures don't happen by accident. Here are the attributes we heard Forum speakers referencing time and again:

- *Listen up, down and out.* Value-centric organizations don't dream up how to deliver value to the customer. They get many of their best ideas from sellers who get them from the customer. Sellers hear, see and sense what excites the customer. Sure, market research plays a role. But in these companies, sellers are the eyes and ears that tune into what customers value. And the company listens closely to its sellers.

- *Force change, allow failure.* Brad Cannon of Medtronic said, "You need a willingness to try new ways to add value and put up with well-meaning mistakes in the interest of serving the customer." Organizations can't succeed in delivering value every time, but it's important to keep trying different ideas. If a well-meaning idea fails, fine. Cut your losses and keep on looking. But always encourage that *value-based entrepreneurial spirit.*

- *Be persistent.* Customers place great value in knowing they can count on their vendors/partners and account managers to deliver what they promise. Mark Toland of Boston Scientific said, "You need to foster a culture that values keeping its commitments." Value-centric companies know this.

- *Hurry, but never rush.* Speed to value counts in today's business environment. "What used to take five years must now be done in 18 months," was how Cannon from Medtronic described it. But he added commentary on the need to get it right through the use of tests and pilots. The value-centric organization moves rapidly, but also moves surely.

- *Encourage healthy paranoia.* Executives in value-centric organizations are always looking over their shoulder. They worry about doing things better and about competitors that offer attractive alternatives. Referring to the ever-changing market in which she operates, Valerie Mason Cunningham of Xerox said, "There can be no complacency when you manage in permanent white water." Executives in value-centric organizations care about doing things better. And they expect their people to feel the same way.

Closing Comments

Value selling is not for every company. Nor is it for every segment.

For companies that simply promote products and prices to grow top-line revenue, the best sales function is one that efficiently delivers messages by leveraging channel partners, inside sales and the Internet.

But for those companies that see growth opportunity in serving customers seeking insight and business process improvement from their vendors and partners, an investment in sales resources that can deliver this value must be a consideration.

If value-seeking customers are an integral part of your sales growth strategy, prepare to make some bold moves. Value selling could be your key to differentiation and success in 2013 and beyond.

SECTION III

Strategic Investment in Sales

Strategic Investment in Sales

NEW JOBS, PROCESSES AND PROGRAMS aren't free. Given the investment required, someone will eventually ask, "Is it worth it?" There needs to be a reasonable ROI argument to back up any request for time, effort and funds. The move to customer-motivated value selling is too important and too much commitment to take on faith. It must make strategic sense. It has to make financial sense, too.

ARTICLES IN THIS SECTION

- Why Invest in Sales?
- Want Growth? Invest in Sales
- Smart Sales Investments

Chapter 7

Why Invest in Sales?

Author:
Gary S. Tubridy
Senior Vice President
The Alexander Group, Inc.

MORE THAN 100 SALES LEADERS met at a recent Chief Sales Executive Forum to discuss the types of investments they are making in their sales organizations to drive revenue growth.

Michael Orrick, senior vice president at Thomson Reuters, summed up the situation in our wrap-up session: "We were so naïve back in 2007 and 2008. We were saying that the revenue was going to come back after the recession. I now see people are talking a lot more about selective opportunities. After that, it's really down to your investment and what you can expect in return."

Even in these hard times, sales leaders are making big bets in their people, from more rigorous approaches to onboarding, to creating roles to actively mentor and coach out in the field, to "taking the training wheels off" by pushing reps not to rely too heavily on specialist resources.

Sales leaders are also putting their ear to the ground to develop formalized programs to collaborate with their customers and push them to think outside the box. Kevin Warren, president of US Customer Operations at Xerox, shared its Dreaming with the Customer program, to get engineers and Xerox customers in the room to brainstorm ideas and solutions. As he noted, "Your competition is out there talking to customers, too. They are offering the same solutions and then you are just competing on price."

Customer expectations have increased. They won't tolerate the "what keeps you up at night" approach to selling anymore. They want reps to act as experts and to be prepared to tell them what other people are doing to solve similar problems. For sales leaders, this translates into a need to develop strategic thinkers who are still able to execute and close deals.

By increasing the intellectual capital of the front-line sales organization, sales takes on more ownership of the customer relationship. Getting that intelligence back to the product development and marketing teams is seen as a key success factor and a critical competitive advantage.

Strategic thinking, more internal and external collaboration, increased use of social networking tools. The sales rep that customers are looking for has to be prepared to act faster, do more with less and be seen as the solution expert. Does your sales organization have what it takes to make the leap to value selling?

What Is Value Selling? Why Does It Matter?

Sales executives from high-tech, media and financial services. The Alexander Group had the opportunity to poll some sales executives on six critical dimensions of value selling:

1. What does *value selling* mean?
2. How large is the *value segment* in your business?

3. How important is the *value segment* to achieving your growth goals?

4. What kind of investments are you making to better cover the *value* segment?

5. How do you plan to reach the C-suite executives who care most about the *value message?*

6. How do you plan to pay for this investment in *value sales* coverage?

What does value selling mean?
Value selling is all about helping the customer make more money.

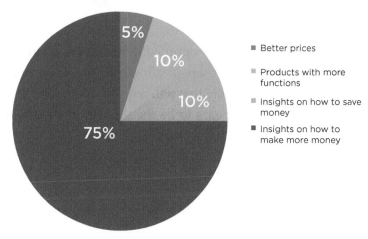

Three-fourths of Forum guests agreed with this point of view. Better prices, better products and advice on how to save money all garnered some votes. However, delivering ideas and insights to help the customer add money to their top line is the heart of what value selling is all about.

How large is the value segment?
The value segment represents less than half the business.

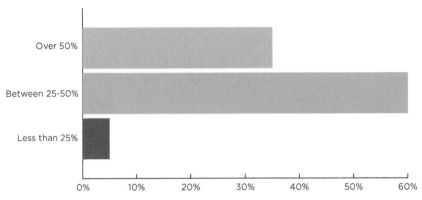

While the value segment is significant, it is by no means dominant. Participants noted that there is still plenty of transaction and product-centric selling out there that will require sales coverage. That said, the value segment appears to be the most important when it comes to achieving *company sales growth objectives.*

How important is it to making your goals?
Extremely important.

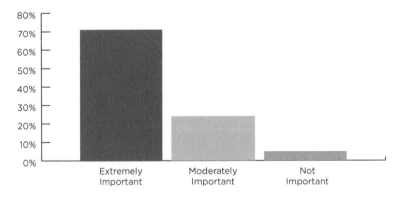

Deeper questioning revealed the reason for the importance of the value segment in meeting growth goals. Companies that inhabit the value segment are as a whole growing faster than their counterparts in the price and product-oriented segments. To leverage this opportunity, sales leaders are planning to ramp up their capability to both *acquire new customers and grow share of current customers* in the higher growth value segment.

What investments are needed to inject more value into the sales process?
Resources that can deliver solutions tuned to specific verticals are by far the most valuable.

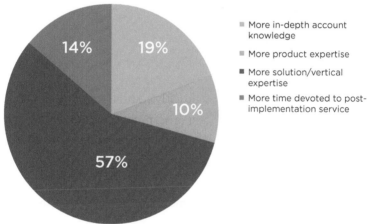

- More in-depth account knowledge
- More product expertise
- More solution/vertical expertise
- More time devoted to post-implementation service

The message from these executives was clear. Deep account understanding is great; post-implementation service is necessary. But if you want to promote your company as a provider of *real value* to the customer, then you had better come prepared for a deep conversation on industry issues, possible solutions and the role you can play in delivering such solutions.

What is the best way to inject the necessary vertical expertise?
Leverage your marketing function to the gretest extent possible.

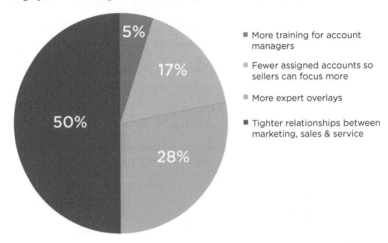

- More training for account managers
- Fewer assigned accounts so sellers can focus more
- More expert overlays
- Tighter relationships between marketing, sales & service

Overlays can add expertise quickly…and expensively. Executives at this Forum believed the fastest (and most efficient) way to deliver expertise to the customer is to find and leverage expertise that already exists in your own company, especially in the marketing function.

What is the best means to deliver value messages to C-suite executives at your customer?
Combine internal executive sponsors with powerful references to get the best access and the most impact.

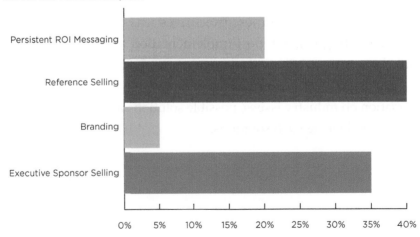

Once again, executives were keen to use resources that are already available. Enlist the vice president of marketing to pay a call on his/her counterpart at the customer to discuss how a new approach to data analysis can affect promotion response. Pull in the vice president of finance to explain the details of a complex ROI model in your proposal. It helps as well to have strong references and cases to bolster claims about performance and ROI. Work closely with marketing to capture the stories that support your case. Keep it fresh by adding new material as often as possible.

Value selling will require some degree of investment. How will this get paid for?
A balanced approach of cost cutting and improving margins is the surest path to success.

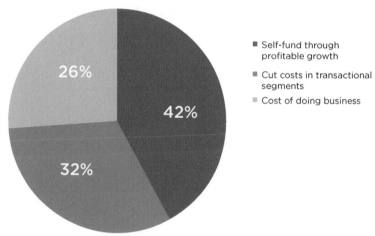

- Self-fund through profitable growth
- Cut costs in transactional segments
- Cost of doing business

Executives agreed that you cannot simply claim that value selling is "a necessary cost of doing business." If you want the company to make the investment in the assets needed to sell and deliver value, plan on delivering *both* higher margins *and* lower coverage costs for segments that require transaction/product-centric selling.

Closing Comments

The executives at this West Coast Forum agree on three key points about selling in today's economy:

1. Say "yes" to value selling. It is the key to achieving your growth objectives.

2. Deepen your expertise in verticals. Customers expect a level of expertise that borders on management consulting. Reaching trusted advisor status is the objective.

3. Leverage the resources at your disposal. Yes, some investment will be needed. But seek out deeper relationships with marketing and other select functional leaders to deepen relationships among high-level executives and decision makers at your accounts.

Chapter 8
Want Growth? Invest in Sales

Author:
Gary S. Tubridy
Senior Vice President
The Alexander Group, Inc.

A RECENT CHIEF SALES EXECUTIVE FORUM explored what top companies are doing to enhance their investments in the sales function from two important perspectives:

- What are top sales executives doing to win more investment dollars for the sales function?
- How are they planning to invest these dollars to maximize return...and the odds of making the numbers next year?

Insights for this summary were gathered from two sources:

- Comments of Forum speakers from both prepared presentations and panels.

- Statistics and comments from the Alexander Group's annual *Sales Pulse Survey*.

This article will summarize the wisdom of leaders from some of the top sales organizations in the world regarding where and how they are investing to position for success.

Smart Sales Investments

Three central themes emerged to form a framework for successful sales investment:

1. *Speakers at the Forum expressed a fundamental belief that there is no better place to invest than in the sales organization.* This belief, tempered by the financial realities of a post-recession world, animates the pursuit of their fair share of available investment dollars.

2. *If you want to invest more, you have to find areas in which to spend less.* Smart executives know that no program lasts forever. They are willing to balance the desire to invest in something new with the toughness to cut that, which no longer produces a great return.

3. *Listening is a high-value/low-cost investment.* When delivering value depends on targeting the right investments, you need all the insight you can get to choose wisely. Listening to customers and to sellers proves to be both a vital source of investment insight and an opportunity to enhance loyalty all around.

Sales Investment Yields Superior Returns

Sales leaders who spoke at the 2011 Forum boldly asserted that if you want results fast, there is no better place to invest than in the sales organization. Michael Orrick, senior vice president at Thomson Reuters, estimated that you can start to see measurable return in as little as six months, far faster than similar bets made in product development or marketing. Even more powerful was the assertion that investment in products and marketing programs are bound to be sub-optimized if related investments are not made in the sales organization. Chris Ancell, senior vice president at CenturyLink, said, "Even today, at most companies, the level of cash on hand is at or near an all-time high. Customers can spend. Good selling will persuade them to do so."

While investment in other functions can take 12 to 36 months to pay off, an investment in sales can pay off in a six to 12 month time-frame. Kevin Warren, president of Xerox North American Operations, was clear: "You can have great brand and product, but if you have the wrong people selling it you are at a disadvantage." All agreed: Concurrent investment in good sellers drives a better return on investments in marketing. In the words of Orrick of Thomson Reuters, an investment in sellers "who can balance the need to understand customers with the ability to challenge them about the possibility of approaching a problem differently" is one of the most attractive short-term investment possibilities for any company.

Investment Opportunities

Executives were eager to assess investment opportunities to help their sellers deliver more value (and differentiation) to the customer, placing them in two basic categories: talent & processes.

Investing to improve sales talent. The following areas of sales human resource development are receiving investment consideration in 2012:

- *Hiring profile.* Who and what type of person to hire has received significant investment at some companies. CenturyLink now uses centrally prescribed hiring criteria and testing processes to ensure the caliber of the individual deployed is consistent with its emerging value-added sales strategy. At HP, they make sure the salesperson profile meets more than just internal standards; they make sure applicants also meet customer needs by including customer interviews in the hiring process. If you don't impress, you don't get the job!

- *Hiring cadence.* In many instances, the number of new hires taken on at any one time is metered to ensure that their numbers do not outstrip the ability of the organization to effectively process them to shorten the onboarding ramp and the time to achieve results. Consistent hiring is better than "lumpy hiring."

- *Training.* Training is back...at least among the companies at the 2011 Forum. Examples abounded. At CenturyLink, there is a half-year program run at corporate that combines work in the field with work in the classroom. HP has invested big time in building "Sales University" where all sellers go through a formal certification process.

- *Coaching.* Standards for first-line manager time devoted to coaching are now common. Many companies are also investing in training for first-line managers to learn how to be better coaches. CenturyLink imbeds a coach in each region who is given the title of sales-effectiveness consultant and who is charged with putting training into action to ensure better uptake and return.

Investing to improve sales processes. Investment in sales processes tended to center on improving the return on sales specialists—a necessary but sometimes risky addition to the sales organization. Three types of specialists were considered:

- *Specialists who enrich the actual selling effort.* Forum speakers were clear that the secret to successful investment here was to understand that pursuing value through specialization is not the same as "a blank check." Said Andrew Holman, former senior vice president at DJO, "If you flood the customer with too many specialists, it just gets confusing. Figure out what customers value, then inject specialists where it makes sense." Invest carefully. Added Bob Guidotti, vice president of Sales Strategy at IBM Software Group, "When you put specialists in the deal, you want them to add rocket power to the process, not act as 'training wheels' for the account manager. Training wheels just add to cost without adding any value." Do your research. Know where specialist value is really needed and inject it judiciously...where it will produce competitive advantage *and* a premium position.

- *Specialists who supplement the post-sale effort.* Specialists need not be customer facing; pricing, post-sale installation...all of this gets done better by specialists who in turn allow sellers to focus more on the customer and the next opportunity. Dave Edmonds, senior vice president at FedEx, described how he invested in bringing legal and financial specialists directly into the sales organization, turning what are sometimes referred to as "the sales prevention functions" into sales team members who look for ways to serve the customer...at a profit. Result: what Edmonds calls a "sales machine" that is designed to deliver both value to the customer and results to FedEx. Less expensive specialists who help get a better return on expensive sellers are a good investment.

- *Inside sales to supplement the field.* Guidotti of IBM (among others) likes the idea of inside sellers teaming up with account managers to "act like wingmen who see what else is going on in the territories, who can prospect and progress opportunities while account managers are focused elsewhere." In a variation on the previous point, less expensive inside seller teammates, who help make outside sellers more productive, are considered a wise investment.

When & How to Deploy Specialists

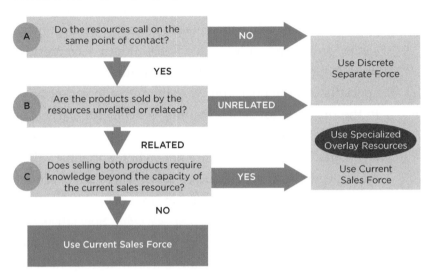

Knowing when and where to deploy specialists and when to phase them out matters deeply. Consider deploying specialists using a series of three "nested" questions as noted below, examining a) similarity of buyers, b) similarity of products and c) seller profiles.

Where You Save Is as Important as Where You Invest

While our Forum speakers champion investment in sales, they are also the first to question whether an investment in sales is getting a good return. If they don't, they know someone else will. The best champion of sales investment knows that it is not about getting more *money*; rather, it is about getting more *return*. As you listen to these executives, you understand that they do not question whether to invest...they are sales champions. But they are very careful about deciding where to put money in and where to take money out. *Decisiveness about where* not *to spend is the key to maximizing investment in places that offer the best returns.*

This theme took many different forms. Orrick of Thomson Reuters said, "Different segments require different solutions *and* different sales organizations." You maximize your investment in coverage by balancing high investment sales approaches for complex situations against lower investment, higher reach sales approaches for transaction selling. He identified three archetypal sales notions. Value selling is expensive to deliver, but worth it when customers are loyal to the sellers (and companies) who "teach" them how to get value from their purchases. Customers who are interested only in transactions produce skinnier margins and should therefore be covered with lower-cost sales resources.

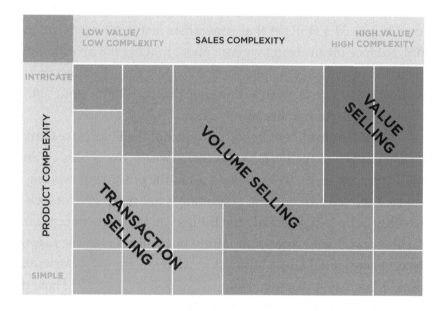

As well, Orrick maintains that a more balanced approach to human resources is frequently needed. Too often, executives overestimate the number of sellers capable of transforming to value selling (in the upper-right corner of the grid). Result: wasted up-front investment in expensive training and coaching to transform sellers who will ultimately terminate. Better to balance the need to transform select sellers with the need to terminate others early and use the funds saved to find more productive replacements.

Guidotti of Sales Strategy at IBM, summed it up when he said, "It's all about balancing customer needs, competitive advantage and profit." This only occurs when you challenge the status quo as it relates to the deployment of expensive specialist resources against market opportunity. "You need to constantly measure the contribution of your specialists. We experiment and take specialists *out* of select sales teams just to see what happens." If price or volume plunges, you have a good case for investing in specialists. If each remains flat, then the expense of the specialist is better invested somewhere else. Where?

"When introducing new products or pursuing new markets, you often need a skill set that generalists just don't have…yet." At IBM, balance means being vigilant about moving the investment in specialist resources to where they will have the most impact and assuming that this is always changing. Said Guidotti, "Your ability to stay agile is your ability to stay ahead."

Paul Mountford, senior vice president of the Enterprise Market at Cisco, spoke to the need to choose between "the genius of 'and' vs. the tyranny of 'or.' That is, don't get in the position of needing to choose between two or more potentially vital programs for lack of funding. Get positioned to do the things you know are important… out of this you will experience failure but will also be able to forge the backbone of the future business in what amounts to a Darwinian form of business evolution. How to avoid such a choice? Have the courage to cut spend on investments that are not delivering a return; force the evolution. Mountford cited Cisco's initial willingness to invest in both emerging and consumer markets, but its ultimate decision to exit the consumer market after it failed to deliver the requisite return. Cisco showed skill on balancing the desire to explore growth opportunities with the need to make "hard-nosed" decisions about what to expand and what to shut down based on the facts. Make choices about where to focus resources based on experience and facts, not on assumptions or the false choice about "either/or."

Balance Generalists and Specialists

How to enhance your ability to stay agile and balance the need for generalists vs. specialists? Noted on the following page is an Alexander

Group model, which illustrates the relationship between generalists and specialists based on assessment of the need for a) product knowledge and b) deep business acumen. Where both product knowledge and deep business acumen are needed, it is easy to exceed the intellectual and physical bandwidth limits of a single individual. Here, some degree of specialization in product is recommended to enhance the account manager's basic understanding of the customer's business. The reward for such investment in added resource should be premium pricing. Conversely, where the need for business acumen outweighs issues in product complexity (as in when product lines mature), it is often both more efficient and more effective to centralize coverage in a single account manager. Where neither business acumen nor product knowledge are valued by the customer (lower left cell in the matrix), it is time to consider lower cost distribution alternatives.

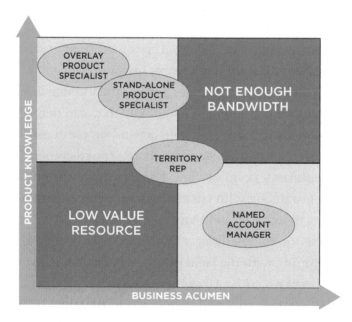

Listening: A High-Value/Low-Cost Investment

Smart sales leaders invest in the means to stay close to the two best sources of investment ideas available to them: customers and sellers.

By listening carefully to each, they not only enrich their understanding of value but also build loyalty as a by-product. Four "listening insights" offered were:

- *Invest in a value dialog with customers.* Be willing to engage in a dialog about the future. Ask "what if….?" At Xerox, such dialog has been institutionalized with programs such as Dreaming with the Customer, where engineers work with customers to elicit ideas and envision products and services that build on these ideas. Want to start a dialog with your customers? Ask them for opinions about what *they* would like to see in an account manager. HP does. HP's large account customers are on the interview list and get a seat at the table when deciding who is going to call on them. At CenturyLink, Ancell tells us they "measure how many customer calls that product people go out on." The aim is to have more than just "a zoo experience where marketers get to look at customers from a safe distance." Like Xerox, CenturyLink wants two-way dialog that produces both insight and ideas. Sales leaders (and through them, sellers) should have an opinion about how they can help customers achieve their goals. That goes beyond simple questioning and the search for understanding. It gets the customers thinking. It requires a point of view. Leaders make sure their sellers create a dialog with customers by having a point of view in areas that matter to them.
- *Invest in a strategic dialog with sellers.* At Xerox, they also have a Dreaming with the Field program to bring sellers and headquarters executives together to envision products, services and coverage that will deliver the most value to customers. According to Warren, sellers need to be "agitators if product development isn't getting them the products that customers need." Sellers become advocates for customers; in effect, they "own the voice of the customer." Sellers, in the words

of Orrick of Thomson Reuters, "need a voice in the product development cycle...and the company needs to find sellers who crave such a role."

- *Invest in innovation.* Said Warren of Xerox, "Sales leadership is charged with creating a culture that treasures dialog, insight and value." Rich Geraffo, senior vice president and managing director, HP Americas, spoke to the need to foster "an innovative organization." Their point is, while good organizations put a premium on operational excellence, great organizations up the ante and include a visionary element that requires leadership to scan the horizons for new ways to add value. That is more than setting aside quiet time to contemplate. It entails putting yourself in a position to hear insights, experience customers and see the frustrations. And then be creative enough to translate all that experience into a deeper understanding of what customers really need and value. Mountford of Cisco said, "Innovation is a function of need." If you believe that, then you must also believe in the importance of making sure that "listening posts" are built in the field and that leaders have the wisdom to take what they hear and translate it into competitive advantage.

- *Invest in recognition.* Find ways to reward and recognize your elite performers. It is not simply about being "coin operated." It involves rewarding both the right behaviors and the right results. Explained Orrick, "One of my best sellers wants input into product development. His approach to sales is very intellectual...this is a part of the reward mix we all have to think about."

Geraffo of HP coined the phrase "manage the 'sell/do' ratio." While it is important to listen to the field, you must also be willing to take action on at least some percentage of the recommendations offered. Investment ideas come in all shapes and sizes; these executives go out of their way to find and to recognize valuable insight from the sellers themselves.

Investing in Social Media

Investment in deploying social media tools was also considered a sound investment to enhance overall sales effectiveness. Access to social media will greatly enhance value selling, according to Dr. Chris Boorman, CMO at Informatica. Said Boorman, "Sales process can be enhanced through better understanding what companies and customers value." This can be more readily ascertained by going beyond the 10K to LinkedIn profiles and employed in both the planning and the execution phases. "Customers indicate what matters to them in these profiles...professionally and sometimes even personally. They expect sellers to have researched this." Said Boorman, "There is no such thing any longer as a cold call. All calls are now warm." While this may now be considered "going the extra mile," such investments will, according to Boorman, soon become table stakes.

Closing Comments

It's all connected. Getting the investment needed to deliver value (and differentiation) through the sales force during tight economic times requires more than just management conviction. It needs some economic proof. Experimentation to better articulate the ROI can provide this, but it is not likely to happen without conviction. And none of the foregoing is likely to succeed without leadership that sets a tone and builds a culture that prizes learning, innovation and salespeople. Sales growth requires investment. The best sales leaders won't wait for someone else to figure out how much; they will figure that out for themselves. They will pursue what they need and cut out what they don't. More than ever, top sales executives will take on the role of sales general manager and through smart investments in sales will lead their organizations in continued growth.

Chapter 9

Smart Sales Investments

Author:
Gary S. Tubridy
Senior Vice President
The Alexander Group, Inc.

THE ALEXANDER GROUP (AGI) ran four Chief Sales Executive Summits attended by sales leaders from 27 leading companies across multiple industries. What follows is a summary of key observations from this Summit Series, which explored *Smart Sales Investments When Growth is Expected and Budgets are Tight.*

There's No Going Back...Value Is Here to Stay

The world of sales has changed. The recent recession introduced an element of sophistication and business savvy among buyers that is not likely to fade anytime soon. Buyers are demanding more value. Sellers can deliver this with either deep discounts or by more creatively applying the products and services they sell to solving customer business problems. If the only way to improve value is to cut price, you don't require an expensive sales force to do it. On the other hand, if the path to value is delivering improved outcomes, then sales expertise is absolutely essential.

This spells opportunity for savvy sales leaders who are busy transforming their sales organizations to deliver more complex value propositions to increasingly sophisticated buyers. This is hinted at in responses to our *2010/2011 Sales Pulse Survey* where participants indicated their primary focus in 2011 would be to:

1. Deliver better solutions.
2. Deploy better sellers.

Summit participants were more definitive, declaring that positioning their sales forces to add greater value was mission critical in 2011. To accomplish this, many Summit executives referred to a need to transform the underlying culture of their sales organization. AGI noted phrases that captured this shift...

FROM...	TO...
"Maximize transaction volume"	"Maximize perceived value and let the volume follow from that"
"Calling on middle managers in procurement who are discount-motivated"	"Calling on functional executives who own problems and are solution-motivated"
"Push product"	"Uncover opportunities to solve problems"
"Take orders"	"Ask questions"

Indeed, AGI sees a transformation to a more customer-motivated culture that:

1. Views the demands of increasingly sophisticated customers as a means to differentiate from the competition.

2. Anticipates customer needs and avoids being reactive.
3. Provokes customers to think differently about an aspect of their business that can be run more effectively.

One executive referred to his objective to promote "disruptive selling"...asking the customer to approach a business problem/process from a different angle, in a way that leverages your products/services and impacts their results meaningfully.

Transformation to a customer-motivated culture notwithstanding, survey results also tell us that investment in sales resources in 2011 will be small, with a median increase of only 1 percent (and this from a thin asset base considering cuts made in 2008/2009). To fund their transformations, sales leaders will need to make "smart moves," looking for savings on one hand while making investments that can go a long way on the other.

Here is what Summit executives told us they were doing.

Stop Wasting Resources on Habitually Poor Investments

Each of these three things could yield significant savings.

1. *Be aggressive with sub-par performers.* Stop wasting time and resources on poor performers. It may sound ruthless, but it may also be the easiest source of investment dollars. Get a read on the kind of talent needed to add value. Act quickly on sellers who have neither the talent nor the results, who are simply not worth investing in. Such sellers damage your brand and may actually be losing you money every day. They are certainly not giving you any bang for your buck.

2. *Stop throwing money at perennially under-performing territories.* Some territories never produce. As one executive described, "These dogpatch territories always churn when young reps realize they cannot make a living there." Well, if you can't make a living there, why keep reassigning it? Recruiting

and onboarding cost money. So do under-utilized sellers. Find other means to cover dogpatch territories…use inside sales, flip them to indirect sales, partner inside and outside sales to allow one seller to cover more ground. Show willingness to change your strategy…dare to innovate.

3. *Stop wasting valuable sales time.* Sellers with "vision and skill" are expensive. Sales leaders need to get maximum leverage from their unique talent. Yet, as sales processes become more complex even the best sellers can get bogged down in longer sales processes, contract complexity, post-sales service and more. What to do? Again—dare to innovate. Expedite business development by teaming expensive outside sales talent with inside business development specialists. Enable customers to serve themselves on routine orders. Improve service efficiency and effectiveness by deploying less costly service specialists. Give account managers access to contracting expertise. With such support, many sales executives find they can "cover the market with fewer, better sellers."

Invest in Low-Cost Ways to Discover Value

These two ideas have the potential for big yield at minimal cost.

1. *Mine the field for ideas to improve effectiveness.* Leverage the thinking of your best sellers. Many companies use sales councils. Most encourage sellers to express themselves on internal blogs. A few make sure the C-suite gets unfiltered access to "top gun" ideas. One company takes a small group of super star sellers and gives them unfettered access to engage top executives in "peer-to-peer" selling to close *big* deals. Such executives are expected to make calls, own issues, support sales efforts and bond with their peers in client accounts. This sales leader said, "One of the best moves we ever made was putting our procurement officer

on the sales team and launching him at the customer's procurement chief. We stopped banging heads, found common ground that only our procurement expert could find and closed good business."

2. *Mine customers, too.* Sales organizations that want insight into value don't wait for a report from marketing…they leverage their access and go direct to the customer. Customer focus groups allow sellers and marketers to observe and interact with thoughtful clients to gain deeper insight into what is really valued in the sales process beyond just product features.

Consider More Significant Investments to Support Value Delivery

The money saved by dealing with poor performers, poor territory designs and poor time management is reinvested in four high-impact areas.

1. *Invest in sellers with "the vision and skills to use products and services to solve customer business problems."* Provocative sellers bring value through specialization in some combination of technology, industry or business function. They bring enough savvy to gain access to functional managers who own real business problems in client accounts. And they keep this access by conceptualizing bundles of products and services, based on deep understanding of the business process, which improve throughput or outcomes for their customer. One executive in business services explained it this way:

   "Our customers in the legal field need better, faster insight based on the latest legal precedent. Broadly, our sales message is improved efficiency and effectiveness. The particulars of how our electronic service is applied to any given law firm will depend on their practice. The skill of the seller is evident in

> *how they configure the product, training and implementation*
> *services in a unique way to deliver maximum client benefit."*

2. *Consider investments in potentially game-changing technology.* The raw materials of value selling are insight and expertise. Executives at the Summits were eager to invest in new technologies that enable sellers to expand their insights and leverage the expertise of the whole company. There were many examples. Some companies use telepresence technology to virtually bring experts into important sales processes in a timely and efficient manner. Still others have implemented cloud-based knowledge sharing systems to give the entire sales force access to industry insights, cutting-edge proposals, tips on competitor positioning and more. One leader has deployed iPads to the field so sellers can access sales tools, collateral and even expertise at the point of customer contact.

3. *Coaching is the fulcrum which successful sales organizations will use to generate transformation leverage.* Summit executives highlighted the extreme importance of first-line managers in driving change through a sales organization. Their ability to deliver hands-on coaching and assessment was seen by all as critical. All recognized the need to first "engage them in the rationale for change" and then to "give them tools to support change." When launching change, most hold special meetings where company leadership lend importance and urgency to the initiative and to the role of the first-line manager. Some spoke of what they called a "coaching boot camp" for new and even more senior line managers to enhance their ability to build rep selling skills. All saw the need for large chunks of line manager time to be devoted to aligning and coaching sellers in their new roles.

4. *Invest in cases, tools and training for sellers to deliver high-impact proposals to C-suite customers.* Assumptions must be reasonable. Models need to be well thought out. Numbers must stand up to scrutiny. But if you have an articulate, defensible ROI message to support a proposal to change the way the customer looks at a process or an issue, you have a powerful tool to win the support of both general and financial managers for doing business based on value, not discounts. Said one executive, "You only get one chance to deliver a message to this level of executive. You have to get it right the first time. If your ROI message holds water, you have a huge advantage over the competition."

Closing Comments

Our unofficial poll of Summit executives yielded little optimism for robust gross domestic product growth in the remainder of 2011 or in 2012. Yet these executives are not waiting for the economy to turn around before they take action. They are taking steps right now to position their companies and their sales organizations to make an impact, to differentiate from the competition and to drive growth despite the sluggish economy.

For most that means stepping up to some form of transformation. Lacking significant transformation budget, these leaders are finding the means to change by implementing a three-part strategy:

1. Cut wasteful spending.
2. Take advantage of easily accessed insights and experience.
3. Spend wisely on programs that help sellers add value to their customers.

But that's not all. Overlaying this strategy, we also noted the importance they attached to nurturing what one executive called "the foundation of a growth culture." This foundation has two notable attributes:

1. *Sales-value vigilance.* The organizations that deliver value best have a cultural imperative that demands "sales-value vigilance…where everyone connected with the customer is always looking for opportunities to add value. Customers don't always know what is possible. Sellers need to help their customers see the possibilities. Moreover, companies need to value the insights that sellers bring back on how to better serve the customer." This means moving from an environment "where sellers hold power by hoarding customer information to one where sellers gain stature by sharing information" to help lift the entire organization. The key here is that top sales organizations are "vigilant for ideas that add value."

2. *Courage to change.* Another executive commented that, in the quest for growth "asking people to change is inevitable. But change is internally disruptive. People don't like it. The organization needs to have the courage to step up to change even if sellers lean against it. You need to have personal courage to manage the change, insist on it and not allow backsliding." The key here is that top sales organization leaders gather the insights, chart the course and keep the organization moving forward despite the forces of inertia.

Sales-value vigilance and the courage to change. Neither represents much out-of-pocket cost on the income statement, yet each is central to finding and implementing ways to add value to customers. Squeeze the discount mentality out of your culture. Make value selling a central component of your sales strategy. You don't have to spend a lot to make a big difference.

SECTION IV
Provisioning for Value

Provisioning for Value

HOW DO YOU ACTUALLY PIVOT from selling things to delivering value through sales? There are many considerations. The role of the seller changes. New specialist positions must be considered. The first-line manager job must be upgraded. Headcount decisions and the ratio of generalists to specialists must be determined. New processes and rules of engagement must be built and implemented. New measures and compensation plans must be conceived and implemented, too. There are a lot of moving parts. And they all need to mesh nicely or the gears will grind to a halt. If you do not provision for value, you will not produce any value.

ARTICLES IN THIS SECTION

- Do Your Salespeople Have Enough Time to Sell Value?
- A New Role for the Sales Manager in Value Selling
- What Is the Right Span of Control for First-Line Sales Managers?
- When Should You Deploy Sales Specialists?
- Predicting the Effectiveness of Sales Support Resources
- Vital Signs of a Sales Force
- Execute Your Sales Vision Through Playbooks
- Sales Compensation in the Value Transformation

Chapter 10

Do Your Salespeople Have Enough Time to Sell Value?

Author:
Paul Vinogradov
Vice President
The Alexander Group, Inc.

ONCE UPON A TIME, a salesperson would make a call on a prospect. The salesperson would arrange a business lunch so the two could get acquainted, exchange business cards and simply learn a little about each other's businesses. The conversation would serve to qualify if there was an interest in meeting again so that the salesperson might ask a few more questions about the prospect's business and share some information about the products the salesperson had to offer. If there was continued interest, the prospect would invite the salesperson to his/her office where they could discuss things in more detail and eventually strike up a deal with an initial order.

Sound quaint? It is. Those days are over. Buyers are more sophisticated, more informed, more time crunched and more demanding than ever. Most buyers are considerably further down the decision process by the time they agree to meet with a salesperson than before. They have already researched their options. They have narrowed their choices. As a result, they have zero patience for sharing information about their company that is readily available to the public. They are willing to take the meeting because they are seeking insights and answers to specific needs and opportunities. A salesperson that secures a meeting with an economic buyer only to launch into a barrage of questions about the buyer's business, or worse, begins spewing information about their products, is swiftly shown the door and not invited back. In many respects, the role of the salesperson has never been harder.

Little time. The average salesperson spends less than 15 percent of his/her time engaging with customers to build relationships and quantify specific opportunities. That may seem surprisingly low, but it shouldn't in light of current trends. Buyers don't have time for this. Salespeople must show up prepared. Every minute counts. The average salesperson spends even less time—just under 10 percent—actually developing solutions, presenting and closing deals. Combined, this amounts to a little over 24 percent of the typical salesperson's time spent doing what we refer to as Engaged Selling, which is a key input metric of sales productivity.

Prospecting	Planning	Engaged Selling	Sales Completion	Other
Generate and evaluate leads	Account planning	Build relationships	Back office	Admin
	Opportunity planning	Quantify opportunities	Order entry	Travel
			Implementation support	Training
	Call planning	Develop and propose solutions	Customer service	Other

How the salesperson is spending the other +75 percent of his/her time is also critical to his/her success. Can some of this time be freed up in order to gain more engaged selling time? Most likely, yes. In fact, top performing sales reps have found ways to work more efficiently and often spend closer to 35 percent in engaged selling. Sales leaders should always be striving to offload unnecessary, low-value activities and coaching to increase focus on engaged selling time. But equally important, if not more important than the *quantity* of engaged selling time, is the *quality* of this precious time the salesperson has with the buyer. They must be prepared, equipped and enabled. They must strategize and plan in order to make every minute of the customer's time valuable. Are they showing up and asking needless questions? Are they pushing products or solutions? Or, are they sharing insights?

Quality time. Planning is one of the most important activities to ensure that the time with the customer is time well spent. As they say, "Failing to plan is planning to fail." The average salesperson spends only 12 percent of his/her time on call planning. Too often, reps are going on calls unprepared or underprepared. While planning time may be less important for transactional, product selling, it is absolutely critical for selling complex solutions. The importance of balancing selling time with planning time has led the Alexander Group (AGI) to develop the Sales Planning Ratio.

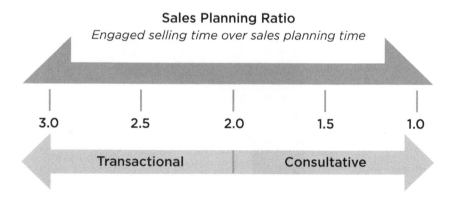

Sales Planning Ratio
Engaged selling time over sales planning time

3.0   2.5   2.0   1.5   1.0

Transactional | Consultative

This ratio helps sales leaders who track sales time to evaluate how well their salespeople are at balancing time between planning and selling. The average rep spends twice as much time (24 percent) on engaged selling as they do on planning (12 percent). If you want your sales force to move toward a more consultative selling approach, your reps need to spend more time planning. This includes more planning at the account level, the opportunity (or deal) level and at the call level. Companies that identify and document their best practices and provide more guidance to their salespeople experience shorter sales cycles, higher quota attainment and nearly 8 percent higher annual revenue growth, according to a recent study by the Aberdeen Group. How much time do your salespeople spend planning? How well-equipped are they at these planning steps?

AGI recently analyzed the responses of more than 25,000 high-tech salespeople to the question: "What is your No. 1 sales inhibitor?" After careful review of their text answers, customer issues surfaced as the No. 1 inhibitor. That's right—salespeople would be so much more productive if it wasn't for those darned customers! This was followed closely by admin and reporting and poor systems/processes. See the following table for a complete list of the Top 10 Sales Productivity Inhibitors.

Top 10 Productivity Inhibitors: High-Tech All Roles

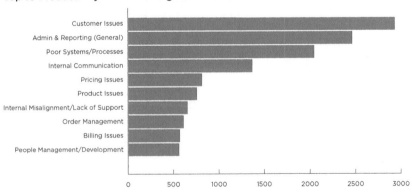

Of course, ignoring customer issues would obviously have detrimental results. Yet, these findings indicate the heavy toll that managing customer issues can have on a salesperson's time and mindset on getting ahead. The common strategy for addressing this problem is often referred to as "Shift and Lift"...Shift the lower cost, post-sale activities to support roles in order to lift the salesperson's productivity by allowing them to focus more on selling.

Closer review of the comments tied to customer issues indicates that these are largely post-sale related issues, including following up on customer issues, resolving customer problems, navigating customer processes, dealing with customer bureaucracy and so on. AGI has seen high-tech companies of all shapes and sizes struggle with this. Solving for it best begins with a benchmarking assessment to determine the "Shift" and "Lift" opportunity. A good assessment will reveal where the biggest productivity improvements exist.

Client Snapshot: One large high-tech company more than doubled its selling time using this approach. The firm moved the average rep selling time from 15 percent to 32 percent. The increase was a result of:

1. Better customer support (+7 percent);
2. Less admin and reporting (+8 percent); and
3. More efficient prospecting (+2 percent).

The company accomplished this gain over the course of 18 months and through careful and thoughtful implementation of several courageous changes.

Chapter 11

A New Role for the Sales Manager in Value Selling

Author:
Linda Mahoney
Vice President
The Alexander Group, Inc.

EXTERNAL FACTORS CONTINUE TO challenge the effectiveness of the traditional sales role. Although they differ by industry, these factors are causing many companies to redesign the role of their sales representative.

This in turn impacts what is expected from the first-line sales manager (FLSM) role. Increasingly, companies are requiring that FLSMs elevate the ability of the sales reps on their teams to make sound business decisions and sell in an increasingly complex environment.

Recently, the Alexander Group had the opportunity to speak with sales leaders at leading companies to discuss the role of the rep in the future and what FLSMs need to do to drive desired change. This white paper highlights what we learned.

The role of the sales rep of the future is illustrated in the following quotes from sales executives:

> "The rep of the future will need to go into accounts and uncover opportunity. Today, they only communicate messages and provide marketing collateral."

> "The really good reps think strategically about their territories and their resources to drive their business. They have the analytical ability and business sense to know where the business is in their territory and to put together a plan to go with it."

Every executive interviewed identified "business acumen" as a key competency that reps need to develop and deepen to be effective in today's environment. While each executive had a different vision of how business acumen was applied, two areas of focus emerged:

1. *Business acumen in a customer-facing environment* where the rep applies knowledge of the customer's business to bring mutually beneficial solutions; and
2. *Business acumen applied to territory management* where the rep identifies where the business opportunities are within their territory and creates a plan to win them.

Formal training and tools can educate reps on the principles of business acumen; however, it is the FLSM that will reinforce and bring this training alive.

This requires that FLSMs change how they execute their role as exemplified by the following quotes:

> "Simply being a coach in the field four days a week is obsolete. Our first-line sales managers need to spend more time planning

with their reps and challenging them on their territory and account plans. It is less about coaching on a specific call."

"Our first-line sales managers need to have a deep understanding of today's business environment. They need to anticipate significant changes versus reacting to them."

"Today's first-line sales managers need to have excellent relationships with their top customers. Our top customers are thousands times more valuable than other customers. We rely on our first-line sales managers to develop deep relationships that are mutually beneficial."

Across the companies we spoke with, the responsibilities of the FLSM tended to align with the following four areas of focus. While these are fairly "traditional" components of the FLSM role, new competencies are required to meet today's execution challenges.

Account Coverage

Approximately half the companies interviewed assign dedicated accounts for their FLSM to cover. This is done for several reasons:

- *Importance of the account.* Several companies noted that there were accounts that were highly influential within and across territories that were not being covered by their national accounts group. In some cases, they found that their reps were delivering "traditional details" to C-level executives within these accounts. At the executive contact level, a deeper needs-based discussion is required.
- *Authority to act.* FLSMs have greater authority to act than their reps and therefore can be more responsive to the needs of key stakeholders within important accounts. Additionally,

they have greater experience and thus are more likely to be comfortable making decisions that require judgment.

- *Maintaining currency.* The competencies required to effectively cover complex accounts will increase in importance. FLSMs with assigned accounts can be more effective in coaching desired behaviors when bringing current experience on needs and how to address them.

Business Manager

Just as there is the expectation that sales reps bring more analytical skills to territory and account coverage, there is increased focus on FLSMs to continually monitor changing industry dynamics and competitor initiatives and proactively identify factors that will impact market share growth. Additionally, it is expected that the FLSM will identify growth opportunities and work with reps to execute the strategies to achieve this growth.

Field Sales Coach

As mentioned previously, expectations for the field rep are changing. Being able to deliver an excellent sales call is important, but seldom sufficient in today's environment. The rep needs to know the business environment and how this impacts top customers. As the economic landscape changes, reps need to examine which accounts they cover and adjust as appropriate.

As a result of the changing role of the rep, the coaching responsibility of the FLSM is shifting from how to deliver a great call to helping the reps analyze their territories, align coverage to emerging influence points and enhance the effectiveness of how reps cover important accounts.

Administrative Responsibilities

While technology, tools and administrative staff can assist in decreasing the time FLSMs devote to administrative responsibilities, it is unlikely that these responsibilities can be eliminated. Recruiting, onboarding, approving expense reports and similar tasks will continue to be a core aspect of the FLSM role.

Optimal Role of the First-Line Sales Manager

Recognizing that FLSMs are essential for any meaningful change to take place in the field, care should be taken to ensure that this role is effectively designed. There are three important considerations: streamline for efficiency, prioritize for alignment and enable for effectiveness.

OPTIMAL FLSM ROLE DESIGN	
Streamline	Systematically understand how FLSMs spend their time. Automate or offload tasks that are low value.
Prioritize	Balance new responsibilities (e.g., account coverage) with available bandwidth. Allow time for coaching. Prioritize to align with business strategy.
Enable	Clarify expectations. Systematically identify and address enablement needs. Provide tools and support. Develop a management system to track results.

Streamline. When designing the optimal FLSM role, it is insightful to examine how time is currently allocated. This examination identifies low-value activities that can be streamlined, offloaded or eliminated. Additionally, the time patterns of high, core and low performers can be analyzed to determine what is feasible and establish goals for how time should be focused. The following chart illustrates time allocation for FLSMs within a typical B2B company. Benchmark averages are called out for comparison.

Prioritize. The FLSM role should be designed to align with and drive the commercial model of the company. For example, if there are a limited number of accounts that strongly influence business results, it may be desirable to assign coverage responsibility for these accounts to FLSMs. Estimating the time required to cover each account ensures that there is time available for coaching and business management. Leveraging other resources to supplement traditional FLSM responsibilities is another alternative. One example of this is to utilize very strong salespeople as peer coaches. This could entail reducing territory size by 20 percent and deploying this time to elevate the capabilities of other reps, removing some coaching responsibility from the FLSM.

Enable. Once the role is defined, it is necessary to assess what is needed for FLSMs to execute successfully. Customized competency models provide a framework to systematically assess individual and systemic gaps that will inhibit execution. Additional tools and processes may be needed to support new requirements of the expanded FLSM role.

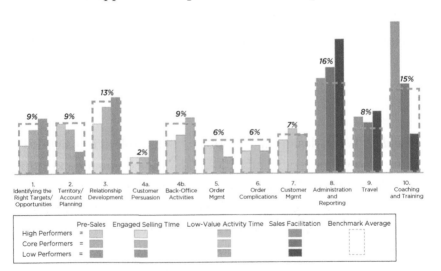

Closing Comments

As the sales environment continues to be impacted by external pressures, companies will need to adapt their commercial sales models. This will require that sales representatives develop and execute new competencies. While training programs can educate and establish expectations, the onus will be on FLSMs to lead the change, coach for desired results and accelerate the change process. Their role must be effectively designed, enabled and monitored to ensure that there is sufficient time to execute high-value activities such as account coverage and coaching, while minimizing low-value administrative tasks.

Chapter 12

What Is the Right Span of Control for First-Line Sales Managers (FLSMs)?

Author:
Paul Vinogradov
Vice President
The Alexander Group, Inc.

YOU ARE IN THE PROCESS OF rolling out your FY13 sales plan and you might be wondering, do you have the right number of first-line sales managers (FLSMs)? What is the right number? In most sales organizations, the FLSMs handle some of the most important tasks and thus have a significant impact on the success of the sales force. They help recruit, onboard, train, coach, develop, co-sell and performance manage the front line. They manage internal communications. They may also manage critical customer relationships. So do you have the right number of them? If you have too few, the ones you have are spread too thin and unable to effectively carry out all these duties. But too many is costly. Trim down the number of FLSMs a little and you easily fund several more reps, increasing your sales capacity.

The average FLSM has 8½ direct reports. But the range is huge, stretching from as few as two to as many as 38. Here are five factors to consider when determining the right span of control for your FLSMs:

1. *Sales channel (field direct, field channel or inside).* Field sales models often require lower spans of control (fewer reps per FLSM) than inside, where day-to-day in-person supervision can allow for 20 percent to 80 percent more reps per manager.

2. *Type of selling (transactional, relationship, solution or partnership).* There is a continuum of four different selling models that increase in complexity, average sales cycle length and average deal size. The FLSM span of control diminishes as these factors increase.

3. *Hiring model (experienced hires vs. college grads).* Sales hiring models vary and, typically, the key difference is the degree of prior selling and industry experience required. Recruiting fresh talent either right out of school or with only few years of experience requires more hands management and training, often on the part of the FLSM, thus a lower span of control is needed than with more experienced hires.

4. *Sales enablement tools and resources.* Simply put, the more help the reps receive through effective tools and sales support resources, the more the FLSM can focus on higher value management activities. The more reps must rely on their own efforts for everything from lead generation to post-sales support, the more involved the managers will be in these activities.

5. *Operational efficiency.* How well-defined and consistently executed is the sales process? Is there a consistent approach to pipeline management? How efficient are the steps for providing customer quotes, configuring solutions, processing

orders, shipping and/or installing solutions and managing customer care? The more efficiently your firm handles the pre- and post-sales processes, the easier it will be for your FLSMs to manage more reps.

Here is a quick guide for B2B sales organizations based on the above factors and the Alexander Group's benchmark database:

SPAN OF CONTROL	LOW	MEDIUM	HIGH
Field Sales	3 to 5	6 to 8	9 to 12
Inside Sales	6 to 8	9 to 12	13 to 18
External Factors	• Very complex sale • Long sales cycle (6+ months) • Very large deals (>$500k)	• Average complexity sale • Average sales cycle (3–6 months) • Average deal size ($50k–$250k)	• Less complex sale • Short sales cycle (1–3 months) • Smaller deals (<$50k)
Internal Factors	• Low sales enablement • Inexperienced hires • Low process and operational efficiency	• Moderate sales enablement • New hires have 2–5 years experience • Moderate process and operational efficiency	• High sales enablement • Highly experienced new hires • High process and operational efficiency

Keep in mind these are guidelines and, while helpful, the best answer will depend on your unique situation. The amount of experience the FLSM has is also a factor. More experienced FLSMs will be able to handle a larger span of control. And, some sales organizations use a player/coach model where the FLSM has a hybrid role both managing reps and also carrying an individual quota. This approach requires a lower span of control.

FLSMs spend an average of 16 percent of their time coaching. That's only four hours in a 40-hour work week. Best practice is nearly double that figure at 28 percent. This delta is driven primarily by internal factors such as operational efficiencies and effective sales enablement. Where does your sales force stand?

Chapter 13

When Should You Deploy Sales Specialists?

Author:
Paul Vinogradov
Vice President
The Alexander Group, Inc.

SALES LEADERS DEPLOY SALES SPECIALISTS to team with their front-line reps to drive additional focus on certain products or solutions—typically newer, more complex and more profitable products or solutions. After all, the average sales rep spends a paltry 3 percent of his/her time each week selling the new product. This is a disconcerting statistic when the sales leader relies on new product sales in order to hit plan. Many sales specialists are the result of acquisitions. When a company makes a strategic acquisition to obtain new technology, it may convert the acquired sales force into an overlay team supporting the core sales team.

But say the word "overlay" and the controversy begins. Finance can't live with overlay specialists. Sales seemingly can't live without them. When do you need them, and for how long? What is the right number? Deploy too many and you'll get buried by double crediting compensation. Have too few and you run the risk of not enough focus on the new, high-margin product, leaving good opportunities overlooked and money on the table.

Understand first that this question begins with job design. Every well-designed sales role has bandwidth constraints defined by three factors: 1) the type of customer called on, 2) the nature of the sales process, and 3) the products and services sold. Sales specialists play an important role in situations where teaming is required to bring the necessary strength of knowledge and support to the sale. When deployed correctly, sales specialists can more than pay for themselves. The trouble is, sales leaders are often in a quandary on how to do it right.

When to use them. Here is a simple decision tree to use when considering deploying sales specialists. Notice how the first three questions map to the three job design factors of customer, process

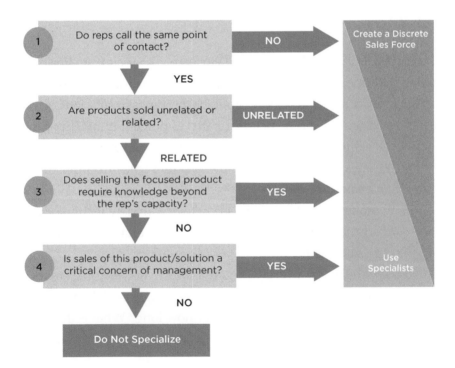

and product. The last question gauges the criticality of the business goals for the product in focus.

Notice also that specialists are designed to team with your existing sales force, hence the word "overlay." However, under certain circumstances, you are best off deploying a separate or discrete sales force. This is generally true when selling unrelated products to a different buyer, or when there is no obvious benefit gained by selling them together.

Generally speaking, sales specialists should be deployed temporarily. Their goal should be to "work themselves out of a job" by training both the sales force and customers on the new offerings. The lifespan of a sales specialist can be as short as six months and as long as five years. Some specialists might stay on far longer if they continue to evolve, shifting their focus over time to newer products.

How many do you need? The right number to deploy depends on the complexity of the sale and the nature of their role. Here is a simple guide to consider when determining the ratio of specialists to your front-line sales reps:

	LOW	MEDIUM	HIGH
Specialist to Rep Ratio	1:8	1:4	1:2
Customer	Single buying contact	Primarily one buyer	Multiple stakeholders
Sales Process	Short, Transactional	Several months, Moderately complex	Up to a year or more, Highly complex
Product in Focus	Product is complementary to existing offerings and solutions	Product is an important element of an integrated solution	Product is an essential part of an integrated, customized solution
Importance of Success	Under evaluation	Highly important	Mission critical

Realize that these are simply guidelines. The answer for your organization may vary based on several factors, including product maturity, sales force experience levels and competitive landscape, among others. We've observed ratios as low as 1:20 and as high as 1:1. An inside-based (phone and Web only) sales specialist can effectively support more field reps. Practically speaking, a field-based sales specialist will struggle to adequately support more than eight sales reps. The average deployment ratio is 1:4. Scenarios with 1:1 are rare and short lived, usually the result of two sales forces merged, but not fully integrated.

Chapter 14

Predicting the Effectiveness of Sales Support Resources

Author:
Ian Zhao
Manager, Benchmarking Services
The Alexander Group, Inc.

For MANY SALES LEADERS, adding support headcount is like walking a tightrope: Too little support may not budge the top line, but too much support could hurt the bottom line. Striking a balance is so tricky because support resources have only an indirect impact on revenue. If one could tell for sure that, say, adding X support headcount would increase revenue by Y dollars, then adding support headcount (or not) would be a snap. As it turns out, it's possible to do just that by leveraging the right sales analytics techniques in three steps.

First, construct two sample groups. Divide your top-performing reps into two groups: an experimental group and a control group. The groups should be large (30+ reps) and similar with regard to demographics and average rep performance (use random assignments to accomplish this). The experimental group will be given the level of sales support that you're considering making available to the entire sales force. The control group will continue with the current support level without change.

Second, collect data. After a short while has passed, gather information on every rep across both groups, including but not limited to:

1. Quota and quota attainment;
2. Pipeline movement;
3. Revenue flow; and
4. Sales activities and time allocations.

Quota, revenue and pipeline information should be easy to obtain, because sales departments track them regularly. Sales activities and time allocations can be captured by the use of a survey.

Third, analyze the data. Compare the groups' results using two statistical methods: hypothesis testing and regression analysis. Hypothesis testing will tell you whether or not the experimental group's performance is significantly different than the control group's; regression analysis goes further to map out the causal relationships between the factors at play (obviously, "whether or not a rep has full sales support" is the most interesting variable here). For a more thorough test, include other variables such as education level, tenure, etc. into your regression analysis.

Of course, these are just general steps. But, eventually, you'll wind up with an equation, which predicts the effect of each variable on overall rep performance. Then you can judge for your organization whether or not adding sales support headcount makes sense.

The Alexander Group (AGI) recently ran these analyses to evaluate the effectiveness of a clinical specialist program for a large medical device company. The client had a traditional "lone wolf" sales model. Sales reps spent much of their time in operating rooms, limiting their ability to field other sales opportunities. In considering whether to offload operating room activities to less expensive clinical specialists, the client brought in AGI to assist the transition. AGI advised the client on a two-phase implementation: First, involve only a small sub-set of sales reps; then if (and only if) the reps' performance improved dramatically, implement a large-scale deployment.

Initial results were encouraging. Reps with clinical specialist support brought in 28 percent more revenue than those without; more than enough to cover the added costs. But revenue increase alone didn't necessarily indicate that the difference was a direct result of the clinical specialists—it may have been due to other factors that set the experimental group apart from the control group.

To investigate, AGI performed a regression analysis, which treated time allocation, tenure and having clinical specialist support or not, as independent variables. The result showed that, after controlling for other differences, a rep with a clinical specialist should bring in $230K more revenue annually than a rep without one. The positive impact of clinical specialists on revenue was loud and clear. The client went ahead with the full-scale implementation, and AGI was retained as an advisor to measure the final result and disembarked on a journey to find the optimal point for sales support.

When it comes to investment decisions, timing is everything. In theory, deciding when to start investing and when to stop should be an informed process. In practice, however, investment decisions rely heavily on intuition and trial and error. The key to making such decisions in a more precise and scientific way…and you may already know what I'm about to say…is through thoughtful, rigorous data analysis.

Adding Sales Support Headcount

Let's return to the earlier topic—deciding whether or not to add sales support headcount to an existing sales force. In this case, it's best to take two distinct measures of performance. The first measure, which was discussed previously, is taken during the initial test phase and is used to predict whether a full-scale implementation will be worthwhile. The second measure, and the focus of this article, takes place after full-scale deployment and sheds light on when to stop investing further, as the optimal point has reached.

As mentioned previously, AGI helped a medical device client decide whether to roll out a clinical specialist program. Once the client had rolled out the program to the entire sales force, it settled on a near 2:1 support ratio, i.e., two sales reps for every clinical specialist. At this point, AGI stepped in to conduct its second measure of performance. AGI found that, while the results of the general deployment were still very positive, the average increase in rep productivity had fallen from our initial measure of $230K (during the test phase) to $180K (sales force-wide implementation). It seems that the law of diminishing returns was at work here. So, should the client stop investing now? Or should they continue ahead full steam, bringing the Customer Service (CS)-Rep ratio all the way to 1:1?

The answer would be found in a time-series analysis of individual rep performances. AGI constructed a panel set of data with two records for every rep: one detailing revenue performance during the experimental period six months prior, and one detailing revenue performance after the full-scale deployment. Using time series regression, AGI calculated that the effect of a clinical specialist on revenue was between $150K and $500K—a wide range indeed. But exactly where in that spectrum the true number lay would determine whether or not to push on with the program.

By isolating the differences *between the two records for the same rep*, AGI created a new set of variables with which to run another regression. The result showed that having CS support should increase a given rep's revenue by an average of $154K. Therefore, AGI advised the client to cease further investment in clinical specialists, as the theoretical benefit of a clinical specialist was fast approaching the actual cost of one.

This serves only as one example of how to gauge when to stop investing in sales resources. Other methods, e.g., regression with data in logarithmic format and maximum likelihood calculation, would have given us the same answer. But when simpler calculations can get the job done, what's the point in show-boating advanced statistical knowledge? To achieve the stated goal using the most efficient method.

Chapter 15
Vital Signs of a Sales Force

Author:
Ian Zhao
Manager, Benchmarking Services
The Alexander Group, Inc.

SALES CONSULTANTS LIKE TO THINK OF themselves as doctors of sales. Yet, a doctor's appointment starts with something easy—taking basic vital signs such as temperature, blood pressure and pulse rate; a consulting project, on the other hand, often kicks off with a long list of data requests—long enough to keep clients wondering if the consultants are trying to boil the ocean.

Let's face it: The up-front data requests are inevitable, since the alternative, piecemeal data collection throughout a project, is even more burdensome and undesirable. However, the Alexander Group does leverage two key measures of sales forces to help eliminate unnecessary data requests: the distributions of rep tenure and quota attainment.

The Alexander Group believes that these are the truest vital signs for a sales force.

Let's talk about tenure first. Everybody knows that average tenure is an indicator of a sales force's experience, but seldom do people think that the histogram of a tenure distribution also reveals turnover information. In fact, this is a trick that anthropologists have been using for decades. To gauge the population growth of a country, they often take a count of the population by age group, producing something like a histogram rotated counterclockwise by 90 degrees. Because of different birth and death rates, those countries with large youth populations are experiencing a baby boom, and those countries with large elderly populations at the top are suffering population decline.

By the same token, histograms of sales reps by tenure that show a gradual decline of rep headcount as tenure increases are indicative of a stable sales force. When a company exhibits an exponential curve with very large numbers of rookies, chances are the sale force is in a rapid expansion. These observations then could tee off an in-depth discussion with the sales leaders on sales growth and sales force development.

Compared to tenure distribution, the distribution of quota attainments is more complicated. Since quota attainment is calculated by dividing revenue by quota, the distributions of the numerator and denominator both affect the distribution of the quotient. In a most simple case, a sales force should have normally distributed quotas, with, for instance, quotas in North Dakota and New York City on opposite tails of the bell curve. If everybody has a fair chance of making quota, the revenue should be normally distributed, as well. When a normally distributed revenue curve is divided by a normally distributed quota curve, the result is a so-called "Cauchy Distribution," with a taller, thinner peak and thicker tails than a standard normal distribution. This is in line with real-world experience. A good quota setting practice should see most reps making (but not exceeding) quotas, resulting in a clustering of reps around 100 percent; hence, the tall peak. But there will always be some reps making 200 percent or even 400 percent of their quotas; hence, the thick tail.

In the real world, however, most quota distributions are not normal and the likelihood of achieving quota is not evenly distributed on either side of 100 percent. As a result, quota attainment distributions will be either right- or left-skewed. By taking a look at the shape of the quota distribution, one can form basic hypotheses as to whether the quotas are set too low or too high, or if there may be issues with territory design.

As you can see, tenure and quota attainment alone can tell very important information regarding sales growth, quota setting practice and performance. These are indeed vital signs for sales forces, and like the vital signs that a nurse may take in a doctor's office, they're easy to collect. Just as a good doctor has the medical knowledge to interpret your results, a good consultant should have the basic statistical knowledge to infer from your sales statistics vital hypotheses for your sales organization.

Chapter 16

Execute Your Sales Vision Through Playbooks

Author:
Kyle Uebelhor
Director
The Alexander Group, Inc.

VISION. ALL GOOD SALES LEADERS HAVE a vision they believe will be successful if executed properly. However, as grand as the vision may be, it's only as good as the leader's ability to see it executed well by his or her entire team. Whether the vision entails shifting from product-oriented to solution-focused selling, leveraging new routes to market, merging sales forces or some other flavor of sales transformation, achieving success requires both a clear vision and a sound management model.

From Good to Great

Sales leaders face many challenges in leading the sales force to effectively execute the vision. Somehow, *great sales leaders get it done.* What is their secret? What are the key differences between good leaders and great ones? At the Alexander Group (AGI), we believe one of the key differences rests with the leader's ability to show the sales force how to be successful—in other words, how to execute the sale. The vision is good at capturing sellers' hearts and imagination, but the majority of the sales force needs concrete guidance.

The Sales Leader's Conundrum

Consider the following patterns and challenges that trip up most sales leaders, or what might be referred to as *the sales leader's conundrum*:

- The sales leader fails to clearly communicate the vision and/or show the sales force how to properly execute.
- The sales force is unable to operationalize the vision, resulting in sellers making up their own strategies on the fly, often with poor results.
- A talent gap expands between top performers who figured out how to be successful and core and bottom performers trying a wide range of approaches.
- Leaders wish they could "clone" their top performers and unlock and share their best practices with the rest of the sales force but don't know how.
- Instead of sharing, top performers "sell" internally to protect their prime accounts, low quotas and high payouts.
- New hires struggle to ramp quickly enough, resulting in high turnover and a growing chasm between the haves and the have-nots.

And, this is just in sales. Gaps also exist between sales and marketing with frequently spotty distribution and uptake of marketing materials. These challenges occur amidst the ever-present pressure to demonstrate immediate results. How can sales leaders break this cycle?

Consider the Power of Playbooks

Imagine everyone in your sales organization executing against one vision. Sellers work from a prescribed set of actions, informed by best practices and the behaviors of top performers in the organization. Likewise, sales leaders know how to coach the sellers to achieve increasingly higher levels of success. Sellers know what marketing materials are available and when in the sales process to best use them, and marketing understands what materials are most effective. If a big transition is coming or underway, everyone in the organization is prepared to adapt and proceeds to change to the new practices in concert.

Sound too good to be true? With sales playbooks, this level of harmony and performance is possible. World-class sales organizations are outpacing their competitors through the use of playbooks. Can you believe the key ingredient that great sales leaders leverage for success is borrowed from the football field? Consider how a football team must drive the ball down field and across the goal line. The guiding force isn't just the coach or the quarterback—it's the playbook. It shows the players how to execute the play. Today's B2B sales environment is marked with increasingly complex and rapidly changing buyer demands. Sales playbooks, more than ever before, can show the sales force how to execute and achieve success.

Turn Tribal Knowledge into Best Practices

A recent Aberdeen Group[1] study reveals that when companies identify and document their best practices they outperform others in three distinct ways. First, they have a *10 percent shorter average sales cycle*— they move more deals through the funnel at a faster rate. Second, they have *4 percent overall higher quota achievement*. Finally, and most importantly, their *top-line revenue growth is higher by nearly 6.5 percent*.

---

[1]   AberdeenGroup. (2012) white paper on Sales Playbooks: How the Best-in-Class Connect Marketing and Sales Through the Entire Selling Lifecycle.

Yet, simply capturing knowledge and documenting it is not enough. How often has an investment in sales aids started collecting dust almost immediately after being created? The secret to getting those best practices adopted is through playbooks, which is why best-in-class organizations are more than twice as likely to have implemented playbooks.

Playbooks can improve engaged selling time by 15 percent. AGI's research shows that a key difference between best-in-class companies and the rest of the pack is engaged selling time. Our sampling of 350 sales organizations and more than 150,000 sellers reveals the average engaged selling time for a rep is 24 percent compared with 35 percent for best-in-class companies. Clients who implement playbooks typically see engaged selling time increase by as much as 15 percent within the first six months of adoption.

Why Now?

Playbooks are not new. Yet, the concept of playbooks is currently having a heyday—a search on Google yields more than a million results, twice as many as six months ago. Why now? AGI believes there are several factors driving the need for sales playbooks:

1. Increased buyer sophistication and accelerated buying processes require salespeople to be more prepared more quickly for every call and every step in the process.
2. Proliferation of multi-channel models—combinations of inside, field, partner, specialist and technical sales roles require greater coordination and collaboration on a single deal.
3. Reductions in new-hire training and onboarding and an over-reliance on self-guided online training methods, leaving new hires guessing.

4. Reductions in the amount of quality coaching and mentoring of reps by their front-line managers whose time is diluted by growing internal demand.
5. Improvements in software that enable real-time, dynamic guidance to the field when they need it.

Types of Playbooks

When does a playbook have the most value to the sales organization? There are several different types and use cases for playbooks. In this paper, we describe four distinct types of playbooks, each designed to meet specific challenges in an organization:

1 Sales Process
- Execution-oriented
- Activity-focused
- Barrier-removal

2 Coaching
- People management
- Region development
- Business improvement

3 Jumpstart
- Transformation primer
- Executive strategy
- Quick wins in a new world

4 Onboarding
- Guide for new hires and their managers
- Acceleration to fully functional
- Tactical and practical

Sales Process Playbooks—The Struggle to Move the Middle

The sales process playbook is the most common playbook type meant to address a basic problem of all sales organizations: a lack of consistent execution throughout the sales force.

The typical bell curve distribution of a sales team's performance indicates opportunity to improve middle performer results by simply adding one or two more deals per year, adding an extra product in each of their deals and decreasing sales cycle time. One or more of these simple improvements can "move the middle" performers a little closer to top performers. Collectively, this movement can drive significant results for the organization. What's the best way to move the middle?

Once again, by capturing and adopting what top sellers do (and when) and translating that into easy-to-understand guideposts. When middle performers replicate the actions of top performers, they improve overall company performance.

Address bottlenecks, anticipate breakdowns. Sales process playbooks can also deliver value when an organization is addressing or anticipating breakdowns in the sales process. Bottlenecks and breakdowns in the sales process occur for a variety of reasons. Common ones include not appropriately qualifying the economic buyer, failing to gain consensus among needed stakeholders or holding onto a "dead deal" too long. However, these breakdowns can often be anticipated when sales leaders are planning ahead for a new product launch or coverage model change. Equipping the sales team to avoid or deftly handle these breakdowns is critical to success.

Sales process playbooks: key performance indicators. A sales process playbook captures and translates the behaviors of top performers, prescribing a set of sales actions designed to guard against common breakdowns in the process. The playbook arms every seller with a consistent approach that ties milestones to key activities and guides the effective use of support resources and marketing collateral. This reduces the amount of improvisation and provides the front-line sales leader a valuable tool to help coach consistent execution across the team. Sales process playbooks help improve:

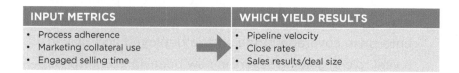

INPUT METRICS	WHICH YIELD RESULTS
• Process adherence • Marketing collateral use • Engaged selling time	• Pipeline velocity • Close rates • Sales results/deal size

Align with Marketing. A key differentiator between best-in-class organizations and others is the alignment between marketing and sales. Marketing organizations within best-in-class companies are more likely to understand sales goals and measure return on marketing investment. Sales playbooks can serve as a vital collaboration tool for marketing and sales. With playbooks, marketing gets a more detailed understanding of the sales process, learning which materials are used when and where, and identifying gaps that require improved messaging. Likewise, sellers understand the role of marketing collateral in supporting their efforts.

CASE STUDY
Fortune 50 Medical Device Company Shifts to Enterprise Sales Solution

The complex medical device landscape is among the most dynamic of any sales environment. Faced with major changes in buyer behavior, huge consolidations, shifts toward integrated delivery networks and group purchasing organizations, this Fortune 50 medical device company needed to overhaul its entire sales process.

A sales process playbook proved to be an essential tool to shift from transactional selling to complex, enterprise-level solution selling.

Initially, the rules of engagement for the new sales model were unclear. The company needed to optimize the collaboration of numerous roles in the enterprise account selling cycle. The Alexander Group worked closely with the company to document the sales motions needed to network above the traditional end-user call points. The playbooks were rolled out in 10 countries as the new enterprise coverage models were deployed and played a vital role in guiding sellers in new behaviors. Enterprise contract wins beat expectations by more than 20 percent in the first 18 months of the new selling model. While sales playbooks cannot be the sole source of that success, the high adoption rates of the new sales process set the company up to win.

Coaching Playbooks—Too Much Juggling, Not Enough Coaching

Perhaps the single most important job role in a sales organization is the front-line sales manager. Deliver the strategy and vision down to the sales teams while simultaneously funneling field-level insights up to executives. Yet, often front-line managers act as super-sellers, promoted based on individual sales results rather than coaching or managing ability.

Front-line managers frequently lack focus. AGI's time benchmarking studies reveal that front-line managers spend too much time in unproductive areas, such as administrative work, rather than on higher value coaching. As a result, sellers are again left finding their way, while the sales force experiences greater inconsistency in execution.

Time to maximize potential. A coaching playbook lays the framework for front-line managers to spend their time on the right activities, condensing and prioritizing what might otherwise seem to be an overwhelming set of tasks. The coaching playbook helps streamline their job and guide them to the activities and behaviors needed for their team's success.

Coaching playbooks: key performance indicators. The value and impact of a coaching playbook can be measured. With a coaching playbook in place, front-line managers can increase their coaching time from the average of 13 percent to best-in-class levels of 23 percent. The real proof, however, is the impact their coaching has on the team, as evidenced by faster ramp-up time, higher productivity and lower voluntary turnover. The success measures for coaching playbooks include:

INPUT METRICS	WHICH YIELD RESULTS
• Coaching time • Onboarding time • Performance improvement plan progress	• Ramp-up time (time to quota) • Revenue per rep • Turnover (voluntary and involuntary)

The primary reason a salesperson leaves his or her job, beyond lack of hope of attaining a goal, is lack of faith in his or her manager to help him or her succeed. Having a good coach's playbook enables front-line managers to mentor and lead sellers resulting in lower turnover of desired sales talent.

CASE STUDY
Redefining the Front-Line Manager's Role

In a leading medical device company, the sales force was facing reduced access to physicians and clinical stakeholders, while needing to increase time in front of administrative decision-makers. These corporate buyers are under high cost pressure, navigating the impact of healthcare reform. The med device company needed to rethink the sales roles to focus time on the right buyers and tasks. The company decided to establish best practices for the front-line managers, who could ensure each team member received the coaching necessary to adopt the new approach.

The first step involved redefining the district manager role. The new role design aimed to reduce super-selling or handling administrative tasks and relationships and increase coaching. The next step involved developing a coaching playbook to provide recommended actions and time allocations for coaching along with tips and tools for managers to find more time for high-value activities. The playbook also offered scripts and guidelines for different engagements with the sales team, including team conference calls, field visits, in-person meetings and one-on-one calls.

The clarified roles, best practices and supporting tools increased manager productivity, enabling them to focus on areas of strategic importance for their district, namely driving more revenue and market share. And with consistent coaching in place, sellers were able to successfully shift to the new relationship model, and overall rep productivity increased.

Jumpstart Playbooks—Facing Transformation

Jumpstart playbooks are specifically designed to galvanize and harmonize sales organizations that face transformation. Whether an organization is undergoing a merger or acquisition or a new go-to-market strategy, jumpstart playbooks provide the focused information that sales teams need to move in a new direction.

> *"The biggest impact from the playbook came through aligning roles and responsibilities for each position within the field sales organization," said Covidien's Kevin Hardage. "While the health-care environment has become more complex, so too has the need for better focus within areas of care of the hospital. The playbook clarifies roles and ensures commercial teams work together as it relates to geographical goals."*

Quick adoption, right out of the gate. Typically, big changes are announced at national meetings. Jumpstart playbooks serve to reinforce the message of leadership as the sales teams return to their daily routines. These concise digests, often just 15 to 20 pages, are designed to ensure quick, consistent adoption of new approaches and new thinking. Sales teams may have process questions—"How am I supposed to interact with this new product specialist that has been placed in my territory?" or "What are the three most important things I need to do today?" These highly focused playbooks are useful in communicating essential information in the critical first 60 to 90 days after rollout of a new strategy.

Jumpstart playbooks: key performance indicators. Sales transformation requires a new set of behaviors that leadership wants to see. Observing and assessing changed behavior is the first measure of success in a transformation initiative. A second important measure is customer satisfaction: How did customers experience the change, and how are we improving our customer relationships?

INPUT METRICS	WHICH YIELD RESULTS
• Practice adoption rates • Sales time improvement • New opportunities	• New product/channel revenue improvement • Customer satisfaction • Net promoter score

CASE STUDY

Software Company Transforms, Jumpstarts Adoption of New Selling Model

A $300M software company faced a constrained market with limited growth potential. The sales organization was struggling with inconsistent sales processes and messaging. The company needed to transform into a world-class selling organization with a much greater emphasis on new customer acquisition.

The Alexander Group developed a detailed implementation and change management plan for this organization, one geared around a team-selling model. This entailed a sales transformation playbook that included several "quick-hit" action steps for sellers. The company announced the sales transformation initiative at the national sales meeting, and the "jumpstart" playbook was rolled out the next day. Sellers assigned to new roles had their jumpstart playbook waiting for them at their desks and/or home offices. This one-two punch approach helped ensure the new desired behaviors would take hold. The sales force realized high adoption from the start, resulting in a more immediate impact and uplift to the business.

Onboarding Playbooks—Accelerate to Fully Functional

Faced with shrinking training budgets and increased demand for real-time results, many of today's sales organizations have eliminated formal week-long (or even month-long) on-site onboarding sessions. Yet proper onboarding requires adequate training on the company, the product, the customer and the sales process. Often, today, a newly hired seller is placed in the field with an account list and a handshake. Their front-line sales managers fulfill the role of an onboarding trainer for most if not all onboarding matters. Onboarding playbooks help guide and accelerate the new hire and his/her coach from the time of offer acceptance through being a fully contributing team member.

Synchronize your talent team resources. Onboarding playbooks coordinate the multiple strategic and administrative efforts needed to make a new seller productive. Best-practice organizations use these guides to leverage the front-line sales leader in the onboarding effort. They act as a "Day 0 to Day xx" guide to orchestrate the modular, self-study training sessions, HR administrative requirements, advancement reviews and coaching cadence.

Onboarding playbooks: key performance indicators. With the cost of non-productivity measured in thousands of dollars per day, the return on onboarding playbooks makes for a logical and easy investment decision.

INPUT METRICS	WHICH YIELD RESULTS
• Onboarding cycle time	• Seller revenue by tenure
• Training advancement	• Sales team retention rate
• Sales training budget	• Sales team engagement/satisfaction

Facilitated Design Yields Quality Playbooks

For many years, the Alexander Group has created playbooks for world-class organizations. Our experience leads us to believe that the best approach to creating effective playbooks is through a series of facilitated design sessions. Conducting three to four structured, half-day sessions over the course of a month with a small group of top performing reps and a few subject matter experts is the best way to unlock the valuable tribal knowledge and best practices that constitute the playbook. We often use the mantras, "don't overthink it" and "keep it simple." These two notions keep the playbook design sessions on track to deliver a high-quality output in an efficient amount of time. This team of advisors helps construct the first playbook, which provides immediate value. But for the playbook to have long-term impact, it must be viewed as a living tool, refined and updated on a frequent basis, evolving and improving over time.

Pulling It All Together Through Automation

The velocity of change in our selling environments is only increasing, and thus so is the challenge of keeping up with change. The next wave of playbooks are automated versions: online playbooks that are updated and refined in real time. Not only do they deliver the right tools and information at the right time, they provide a real-time, dynamic feedback loop between sales teams, CRM and business intelligence systems and sales and marketing leadership.

Automated playbooks are built on dynamic business logic, so they can deliver even more relevant information and specific plays based on the intelligence in the company's CRM system. Because these automated playbooks are interactive applications, they allow salespeople to navigate more easily through complex information right when they need it. Playbooks can now be mobile-enabled so sellers have needed information with them on the go.

Dynamic interactive playbooks put the right intelligence in the right hands at the right time. Sellers can access deal-specific guidance, and executives can access far more meaningful intelligence on process adherence, collateral usage and pipeline data.

Closing Comments

Whether you need to "move the middle" toward higher performance, empower front-line mangers to coach or prime the pump for a sales transformation, playbooks are an essential means to execute your vision. If you are considering using playbooks, keep these seven simple goals in mind:

1. Diversify your design team.
2. Use an iterative design process.
3. Remember: "By the seller for the seller."
4. Include influencers and successful practitioners.
5. Do not plan on one-and-done—playbooks evolve.
6. Embed into your sales planning and coaching culture.
7. Celebrate adoption; make it a part of the daily routine.

Chapter 17

Sales Compensation in the Value Transformation

Author:
David Cichelli
Senior Vice President
The Alexander Group, Inc.

SALES DEPARTMENTS SERVE two constituents. The first group is the product divisions. They want the sales department to represent their product family fully to the second set of constituents: customers. In short, here is what sales departments do: They define, select and deploy the right sales modality to connect these two sometimes aligned, sometimes disparate constituents—product divisions and customers.

What is the right sales modality? It depends on the variables inherent in both the product offering and the needs of customers. The role of the sales function can range from simply making well-known products available, all the way up to working with the customer until the customer successfully adopts a new custom-crafted solution. The charter of the sales function will vary by the types of products and buyers. Some customers will want ease of purchase; others need purchase coaxing; and others need deep expertise to solve complex problems.

The extent of value-added selling—from minimal to extensive—will affect sales job design, sales performance measures and compensation plan design. A sales job that simply provides product availability will differ in content, measurement and pay when compared to jobs that substantially add value to the company's offerings by creating custom solutions to meet unique customer challenges.

We will examine how the extent of "value-added" to company offerings affects job design, performance measurement and sales compensation plans.

Sales Charter

The extent of value-added selling contained within the charter of a sales job can range from minimal to extensive. This is not a judgment of bad or good. It is a decision of what is the most appropriate selling modality—the level of value-added selling given the nature of the offerings and the types of buyers. Sales management considers these variables when making studied judgments to configure sales jobs.

A sales job primarily serves one of three broad sales charters as displayed in the following table:

SALES CHARTER	SALES FULFILLMENT	SALES ADVOCACY	SALES CO-PARTNERING
Value-Add	Execution Excellence	Decision Guidance	Functional Advancement
	Choice Options	Offering Assurance	Insight-Led Solutions
	Relationship Development	Purchase Justification	New Platform Adoption

Below is a description of each sales charter.

- *Fulfillment selling.* Sales Fulfillment is the act of giving customers access to products with a no-hassle sales process. With some sectors, customers are so well informed of their purchase preferences they can order products without the involvement of sales personnel such as via the Web. In cases where sales personnel are necessary to help customers make known purchases, the extent of value-added selling is minimal. These minimal sales-value selling activities include ease of purchase, choice awareness and strong relationship efforts for repeat customers.

- *Advocacy selling.* More value-added selling skills are necessary to help uncertain customers make purchase decisions. This includes providing education and advice. Often, for the purchase decision to move forward, the salesperson must fully address the anxious customer's downside risks. Finally, for major purchases, a convincing return on investment (ROI) rationale will contribute to an affirmative decision to make a substantial purchase.

- *Co-partnering selling.* Higher sales-value investments are necessary when customers have to replace current solutions with new enablement offerings. The adoption of new functional competencies must frequently overcome the merits of the current practices—even when obvious shortcomings are plaguing such practices. In other cases, the sales team must employ insight-led led selling to create an exceptional solution to address the customer's unique problem. Finally, the top value-added selling efforts occur when the sales team helps their customer—now partner—to define, configure and successfully adopt a new, integral solution—often featuring a major paradigm-shift for the customer.

Each sales charter: Fulfillment, advocacy and co-partnering require an increasing level of value-added selling investments.

Sales Jobs

Sales jobs are the vehicle to connect product divisions' offerings with customers. The nature of the sales job will differ depending on the extent of required value-added selling. Let's look at the three previously profiled sales charters and examine the job types available to help make each sales charter type work effectively.

- *Sales fulfillment jobs.* Most sales entities use classic sales jobs such as territory representatives, account managers and customer service managers to fulfill customer-purchasing needs. When customers know what they want, they inquire about the latest products available, what choices they have and assurance they will get their product/solution in a timely fashion supported by high customer service execution. For those with ongoing purchasing requirements, they would expect enhanced customer support such as frequent sales rep visits, on-site resources, tele-customer support or one-to-one Web support. Often, these customers welcome relationship-building efforts by the vendor and its sales personnel.
- *Sales advocacy jobs.* Moving up the value-added selling ladder, companies will often use the same job titles employed in sales advocacy as sales fulfillment. Again, these titles include territory representatives, account managers and customer service managers. However, the advocacy charter requires more selling persuasion than simply fulfillment. For example, account managers will provide decision guidance to customers helping weigh the pros and cons of various solutions. Key account managers or corporate account managers provide purchase assurance and risk reduction advice as customers navigate purchase decisions. As part of these sales efforts,

providing realistic and compelling return on investment (ROI) pro forma helps buyers justify their purchase.

Sales management frequently adds more jobs to support sales advocacy selling challenges. One such job is the product overlay specialist. When account managers need advanced technical knowledge or application explanation, the product overlay specialist will educate and explain the virtues of the solution. The specialist will also help reduce customer risk and uncertainty. The overlay specialist will champion the solution and provide reference examples of success. Another sales advocacy job is the new account seller. As markets mature, separating new accounts from existing accounts creates a high-persuasion seller role: the new-account business development specialist. These sellers focus on hard-to-win noncustomers. Vertical specialists bring another form of specialized knowledge to the sales advocacy role: industry specific application of the product/solution. Next, pre-sales specialists bring assessment skills and technical integration solutions for complex applications. Finally, partner managers exert their influence by increasing performance accountability of channel partners, establishing standards, training partner personnel and, where appropriate, calling on end-users to promote company sales through the channel.

- *Sales co-partnering jobs.* Adding to the list of job functions found in the fulfillment and the advocacy selling charters is the emergence of problem solvers necessary for successful sales co-partnering. Not all companies need this level of value-added selling resources. Moreover, pursuing sales co-partnering opportunities does not negate the role of sales fulfillment and sales advocacy. However, when customer challenges are significant and their need for deep, comprehensive solutions are evident, then sales co-partnering talent provides the necessary creative insight to help solve the customers' most vexing challenges. The selling bias shifts from presenting the company's offerings as a plausible solution to solving the customer's unique problem by building a multi-dimension, and often, shared solution. In some cases, the selling company will take shared accountability for the customer's outcomes. The selling focus tilts to extensive discovery efforts, assembling disparate solutions, modeling potential outcomes and providing strong change management support for solution adoption purposes. Subject matter experts, such as architect consultants and center of excellence resources, help envision and craft the go-forward solution. Market-sector specialists provide a forward look at the strategic nature of the customer's challenges. Global strategists help broaden and define the worldwide context of the customer's challenge and potential paradigm-changing solutions. Finally, for large, significant opportunities, sales leadership might assign pursuit teams with project management talent to diagnose, craft and deploy customer-unique solutions.

As value-added selling needs increase, the types and diversity of customer contact resources change, too. This evolution of sales value-added efforts needs constant evaluation. Changes in the company offerings and buyer opportunities will often necessitate changes in the sales deployment model to correctly apply the right level of value-added selling investments.

Performance Measurement

Sales performance improves when sales measurement matches sales accountability. Ultimately, all sales efforts must lead to profitable revenue. Any measure of sales success—fulfillment, advocacy and co-partnering—should have a measure of sales results. However, as value-added selling efforts increase, additional and different measures emerge. Of consequence is the movement of measures from primarily company results to a greater focus on customer outcomes. These two classes of measures are not mutually exclusive and can co-exist in a sales measurement system. As the need for value-added selling increases, so does the need to measure and account for customer outcomes. Customer outcome is the essence of sales co-partnering.

Sales results include such classic measures as sales volume, gross margin, product mix, new account sales and other company measures. Sales outcome metrics measure the purchased solution's impact on customer performance, including metrics such as customer sales results, customer cost reductions, customer service levels, customer process improvement and other customer-centric measures of success. Further, when the company assumes responsibility for a customer function, then management needs to link performance measurement to the success of this assigned responsibility.

Compensation

The nature of value-added selling affects the compensation program for customer contact personnel. While sales modalities feature different levels of value-added selling, all compensation programs will prominently feature an incentive for sales production. The second and third performance measure of the compensation program reflects the nature of value-added selling in the job. For sales fulfillment selling, sales compensation programs reward sales execution and customer service measures. Sales advocacy selling primarily rewards sales results. Customer outcomes play a substantial role when compensating co-partnering selling.

Fulfillment selling is the discipline of getting the defined sales process and customer support model correct. Target pay is usually in the lower third of total compensation levels among all sales jobs. Pay mix, the ratio of base pay to target incentive, may reflect 75/25 with 75 percent of the target total pay granted in base pay and 25 percent of the target total pay offered for achievement of expected performance. Upside earnings could be up to 3X the target pay for the most proficient performers. In addition to sales results, service execution and customer satisfaction may be important secondary measures rewarded by the compensation program.

Advocacy selling begins with rewarding sales results, too, but adds additional measures for strategic sales results such as sales profitability, product mix and new account selling. Target total compensation levels are consistent with the middle third of sales professional compensation levels. Pay mixes are more aggressive than fulfillment selling and favor 70/30 or 60/40. Upside earning opportunities usually, provide the same 3X the target incentive amount for the top performers as with fulfillment selling. In addition to sales production and strategic sales measures, the incentive plan might include customer loyalty for sales jobs with ongoing sales to existing customers.

Sales co-partnering jobs often provide the highest target compensation levels in the sales profession. For long sales-cycle selling, sales management may use a more modest pay mix than for fulfillment and advocacy selling. A pay mix of 80/20 might be more appropriate. The incentive plan will make less use of quota or commission formulas and may use contract-signing awards based on contract size and terms. Upside potential may be similar to management bonus programs of 2X the target incentive. Quantitative and qualitative customer outcomes will affect the incentive payout, too. The incentive plan will reward team performance for team-selling results. Ongoing customer success and long-term revenue growth will earn the highest incentive payments.

Summary

Value-added selling, from minimal to extensive, affects the nature of selling, the content of the job, the preferred performance metrics and the design of the compensation program. Ensure that you configure your sales management programs to align with the extent and nature of the value-added selling required of the sales job.

SECTION V

Charting the
Course to Value

Charting the Course to Value

THE IMPORTANCE OF MANAGING change cannot be underestimated. Consider who needs to buy into the pivot to value: senior executives, sales executives at all levels, peers in marketing and service…and, of course, the sellers themselves. Don't give anyone the impression that if they wait it out, "this too shall pass." Give them the unambiguous message that change is coming and they can benefit from it. Give everyone powerful reasons to engage and support the change, because it is good for the business and it is good for them.

ARTICLES IN THIS SECTION

- Harness Culture to Propel Transformation
- Travel Tips on the Journey to Selling Value
- Make Change Your Secret Weapon
- Navigating the Transformation to Value Selling

Chapter 18
Harness Culture to Propel Transformation

Author:
Gary S. Tubridy
Senior Vice President
The Alexander Group, Inc.

Each year, the Alexander Group (AGI) runs the Chief Sales Executive (CSE) Summit Series to explore contemporary issues and discuss possible solutions. Lately, we've heard a lot about value selling as a way to drive top-line growth; give customers a solution to their business problems and they will buy more. That sounds reasonable. But selling solutions is a long way from what many companies are doing today as they focus primarily on selling products and things, not ROI. For most, pivoting to a solution sales strategy will be a major shift.

Recently, AGI explored the critical role of sales force culture in successfully implementing a new sales strategy. Executives from industries as diverse as cloud software to building products participated. They all had two things in common:

1. They needed their sales forces to shift toward value selling.
2. They were seeking insights into how best to harness sales culture to achieve this shift.

This paper describes the combined wisdom of the participating Summit executives on what must be done to update and leverage culture to greatly improve the odds of success when implementing a new sales strategy.

Sales Force Evolution

When moving a veteran sales organization toward value selling, companies are asking a lot. Consider the following:

Sales organizations follow an evolutionary path. In their early stages, when products are new and the customer base is thin, most selling falls into what might be called "missionary selling," meaning sellers must bring "religion" to new customers convincing them to

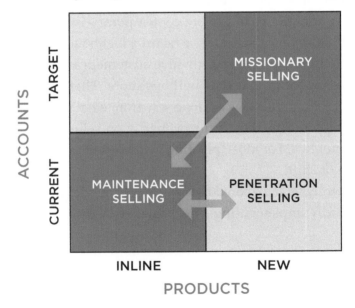

buy untried products from an untried company. This requires missionary zeal as pictured in the upper right of the preceding chart. Now, fast forward two or three years. If the company and its sellers have succeeded, a more veteran sales force is now protecting an account base, which produces solid if unspectacular growth. In the process, sellers are transformed from missionary zealots to "farmers" whose chief responsibility is keeping customers satisfied and loyal (lower-left quadrant).

Over time, new competitors emerge, new technologies challenge old approaches and formerly complacent customers grow in sophistication. To address these threats and re-ignite the growth engine, new products are launched and sellers are asked to a) dive back into the missionary role and b) leverage their relationships to more deeply penetrate current accounts with holistic solutions comprised of both in-line and new products (lower-right quadrant). And, of course, continue keeping current customers satisfied. In other words, operate in *all* sectors of the grid.

All this might make great sense to marketing, but galvanizing a sales force to adopt a new approach and abandon a model that led to past success is a huge request. As one executive stated, "In organizations that are proud of their past and distrustful of change, you have got to take culture head-on and leverage it." Said another, "If you want radical change in your strategy, then you are going to have to step up to driving some change in your culture, too." If you want to change strategy, then you must update your culture.

The Following Definition of 'Sales Force Culture' was Used at the Summit:

Sales force culture is a self-perpetuating pattern of beliefs, thinking and behaviors where:

1. Beliefs embody what sellers understand the business model to be and their role in executing it.

2. Thinking is forged by what sellers are told to do and what they see it takes to succeed in their jobs.
3. Behaviors are the actions sellers actually take as a result of their beliefs and thinking.

Executives at the Summit noted the tendency to lean mostly on programs (e.g., training, compensation) to drive implementation of a new sales strategy. As one said, such programs are "necessary but not sufficient."

While programs attempt to get at the behavioral part of the cultural equation, they do not begin to address what sellers believe their role to be or what they think will actually work. Absent change in beliefs and thinking, selling behavior tends to backslide after the initial push when programs alone carry the burden for change.

If culture is the summation of these three things…a self-perpetuating set of beliefs, thinking and behaviors…then all three must be addressed systematically to produce any significant change in how sellers go about doing their jobs. This is hard to do, but long-term success of any strategy depends on it.

All of this, of course takes time, attention to detail, candor and persistence. Yet, if the experience of the Summit executives can be generalized, it is precisely what is required to harness culture in the interest of transforming both strategy and the sales organization.

Harnessing Culture to Drive Change

A three-part game plan emerged among Summit executives regarding how to harness culture to drive sales strategy change.

1. *Tackle beliefs.* Most sellers want to believe that their company's business model is sound and that the prevailing hierarchy is making wise choices to keep it that way. If you want them to change their beliefs about the business model and their role in it, be prepared to provide a sound explanation. More than most sales reps sense when

they are losing the competitive edge and want to know that this is being addressed.

Said one executive, "People starving for a change want to eliminate uncertainty…they want to know. They sense the need for change early on from their experience with customers. They are prepared to listen." In the words of another, upon learning about a change in direction, sellers often respond with quotes like, "Thank God, we were waiting for something like this!"

Where does such messaging start? From the top. As one executive reported, "It is hard for sales to lead a customer-centric transformation if top management, from the president on down, is not behind it." Building on this comment, another executive added, "It is not just about sales strategy. How we go-to-market must be an outgrowth of company strategy." Make it the CEO's business to speak personally to the sales organization. Send the message down the management chain clearly and consistently, using executives one or two levels up to deliver it to each successive group.

Messaging is more than speeches. To get the message out in a way that impacts the fundamental beliefs of the organization, executives at the Summit stressed the need for regular and frequent informal communication. This included executive forays into the field to be seen, to be heard and to listen to sellers and customers alike. Activities included formal meetings/speeches, but many executives stressed the importance of informal dinner and cafeteria gatherings to "speak directly, from the heart, about why the change matters to the company and to the people." There is no substitute for hearing from an executive three levels up speaking with conviction about the importance of change in your role.

2. *Change their thinking.* Said one executive, if you want sellers to act differently, "you have to change their thinking about what they are expected to do…even allowed to do."

Three actions were noted:

- In the words of one executive, "You have to change what the seller thinks is important to the customer. In our case, we had to convince them to move away from pushing products toward delivering value." How do you make a convincing case for change?
- Try piloting a whole new way of selling. The executives we spoke with advocated using a geographic territory or a segment and involving as many field sales "thought leaders" as possible to test out new ideas. Said one executive, using thought leaders "not only helps convince other sellers, it helps fine-tune the very systems you are piloting." Success breeds success. Said another executive, "Most people are able to change their thinking when they see a new way of doing things...that works." A well-run pilot can turn thought leaders into acolytes and offer strong proof of concept.
- Give sellers and field managers the decision rights they need to succeed. Executives agreed that in many companies too much authority had devolved to corporate, leaving sellers unsure about what they could do in the interest of serving the customer. Clarify what they have authority to do regarding pricing, terms and commitment of resources. And make it equally clear what they do not have authority for. Add to this the spirit for "serving the customer and a willingness to tolerate or even celebrate mistakes if they are made in the interest of delivering value and building loyalty." According to the Summit executives, most sellers will be happy to take the baton and run hard in the interest of serving the customer and making their numbers. Just tell them what the rules are.

3. *Enable Behavioral Change.* Enablement is about giving sellers and managers the tools to implement the sales roles they have been hearing so much about. Quite literally, this is "putting your money where your mouth is." Enablement tools cited were:

- *Compensation.* It is hard "to keep the customer's best interests in mind when your pay depends on the next close." Solution sellers need metrics and compensation plans designed to reward success over the longer term, not just month to month. Said one executive, "See that your compensation plans are tailored to reward the behaviors you are asking for."
- *Coaching.* "Nothing happens until the first-line manager makes it happen." Give these managers the time, tools, training and direction to devote more energy to coaching than any other aspect of their job and "you will get the change you want." As another executive stated, "For these positions, coaching is job one."
- *Recognition.* Find people doing things right and put them up on a pedestal so others can see what a job well done looks like. Find new heroes and role models. According to one executive, while "compensation is important, recognition is absolutely critical."

Hallmarks of Sustained High-Performance Cultures

Out of the Summit discussions emerged the hallmarks of a kind of sales culture that would embrace and accelerate change. Prominent among these characteristics were:

Healthy paranoia. This is a tone set by management that rests just behind the culture of recognition. Even in the middle of celebrating success, executives at these winning companies feel a certain discomfort about "what happens next?" At heart, they are balancing the need to recognize today with the need to avoid complacency tomorrow. By always looking over their shoulder and wondering if someone is gaining on them, these executives are never caught by surprise.

Listening up, down and out. The flip side of telling the troops what you expect is a willingness to listen. Listening to field managers, sellers and customers to find out what works as well as what does not. People want the boss to listen. It validates them. As one executive described, "It is important to involve your people in the vision." Pragmatically, some of the best insights into value come from the bottom up, from sellers who "hear, see and sense what excites the customer."

Frequent, small changes…and a few failures. Evolution produces the best organism by trying lots of small changes to find out which ones work best. The same concept holds for winning sales organizations. You hear lots about pilots, skunk works and trials all in the spirit of trying new coverage techniques, value props or metrics to see if they work. These organizations are also willing to suffer failure (quickly) in the interest of finding value. Said one executive, you need "a willingness to try new ways to add value and put up with well-meaning mistakes in the interest of serving the customer." In these organizations, more change means less complacency.

Trust. Trust comes in a couple of different flavors. Said one executive, "New rules without a strong relationship with the company will not work." Said another, "No one takes any risks unless they know the organization has their back." From this perspective, it is necessary to trust that the management hierarchy will be supportive. From another perspective, there must be sufficient trust in management that the strategy selected is the right one…that it will help both seller and company prevail against the competition. Such trust is frequently the by-product of "frequent communication and open dialog."

Persistence. These cultures frown upon "changing with the wind." Persistence is the flip side of trust…these organizations foster a culture that keeps its commitments.

Speed. "What used to take five years must now be done in 18 months." Said another executive, in our business "we hurry, but never rush." Get the strategy right. Run a pilot to work out the kinks. Then scale quickly. The best cultures understand the need for speed and have a tendency to get things done today instead of waiting till tomorrow.

Understanding the importance of line managers. "Nothing happens until the line manager makes it happen." That is not an isolated statement. You hear it all the time. Organizations with cultures that celebrate and enable the crucial role of the line manager simply manage change better.

Closing Comments

In his statement, "culture eats strategy for breakfast," Peter Drucker implies that you cannot change culture but can only harness it. Summit executives would agree that it is unwise to embark on a strategy that *depends* on vast cultural change. But they would also say it is naïve to think you can drive a significant change in strategy *without* instigating some change in culture. Consider what Lou Gerstner Jr., retired CEO of IBM, said about culture in his book *Who Says Elephants Can't Dance?*

> "…culture isn't just one aspect of the game—it is the game. In the end, an organization is nothing more than the collective capacity of its people to create value."

It's well known that Gerstner changed significant elements of one of the strongest sales cultures in the history of business. If you want to pivot to customer-centric value selling, then you need to start thinking about your sales culture.

Change is possible. Consider the process outlined here...tackle beliefs, change thinking and enable change. It's a good place to start.

Chapter 19

Travel Tips on the Journey to Selling Value

Author:
Gary S. Tubridy
Senior Vice President
The Alexander Group, Inc.

AT A RECENT Chief Sales Executive (CSE) Forum, the Alexander Group gathered more than 70 senior sales leaders in San Francisco and New York to explore the growing importance of value selling.

In keynote addresses, workshops, surveys and in-depth interviews, we heard several common themes:

- *Winning is harder.* Buyers are more prepared and informed, and sellers must bring more than simple product information to the table.
- *Decisions are made earlier.* Informed buyers often make up their minds before even soliciting bids, making many RFPs a waste of time.

- *Pressure to discount is growing.* Absent meaningful differentiation between similar product offerings, the only way to win business is through price discounting.

Under these conditions, the role of the sales force can be either diminished or enhanced. The role is diminished if interactions with well-informed buyers are allowed to devolve to simple price negotiations. This type of interaction may as well be done better and cheaper over the telephone or through the Internet.

But the role of sales is enhanced significantly if sellers can actually inject and deliver value through the sales process—the kind of value that differentiates a product or service offering and commands a premium.

The crucial question is not whether value selling makes sense. It does! The question that looms is how best to build value-selling capability. It is just too easy to assert that value selling depends on deploying the right resources...specialists in verticals, technologies or solutions. True, specialists will be needed. But getting value selling right requires deeper exploration of questions several layers beyond that:

1. How is value selling different from product selling?
2. Why does value selling matter?
3. What type of company should consider value selling?
4. Where does value selling resonate?
5. Can you deliver value through sales at a profit?

The following white paper offers opinions on each of these questions based on observations and insights derived from these Forums.

How Is Value Selling Different from Product Selling?

Value selling is best distinguished from product selling by contrasting the two along four basic sales dimensions:

DIMENSION	PRODUCT-CENTRIC SELLING	VALUE SELLING
1. Message	Centers on product features and how they differ from the competition.	Centers on what the product or products do that enables the customer to improve an important business process.
2. Depth	Seller is expected to know everything about the product and be well-versed in what makes it better than similar competitive offerings.	Seller is expected to understand how the customer makes money, which processes are critical to maximizing results and which are often problematic.
3. Process	Sellers target historical decision makers in middle management frequently and are frequently deflected to procurement. Focus on maximum sales process efficiency.	Sellers target executives in charge of results with whom the process improvement message will resonate. Care about delivering the right messages with the right research to the right people.
4. Results	Seller has little or no attachment to business outcomes; is a guarantor primarily of price and delivery dates.	Seller is strongly connected to the business outcomes enabled by products and processes. Helps deliver promised results to ensure an ongoing, business-based relationship.

In a nutshell, value selling is built around delivering new messages, based on deep knowledge, to higher level buyers through a more complex sales cycle that carries the promise of better results for customers who are open to good advice. Value selling has the potential to produce larger, more profitable deals, as well as more loyal customers.

Why Does Value Selling Matter?

We polled the audience of more than 70 executives with a series of questions. One of the first questions asked was, "What percent of customers actually care about value as opposed to cost?" The response was revealing.

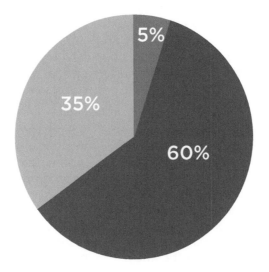

Thirty-five percent of the executives said that value buyers represent more than half their addressable market. Nearly 95 percent indicated *that value-conscious customers make up more than 25 percent of their addressable market.* The value segment is large…in some cases very large.

The follow-up question to this was, "How important is the value segment to achieving your growth objective in 2013?" The answer was overwhelmingly positive:

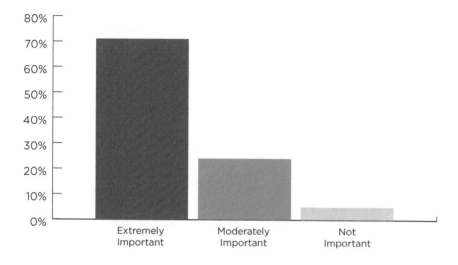

More than 70 percent of participants indicated that the value segment is "extremely important" to the growth objective. Why? One executive summed it up nicely by saying, "These customers are simply growing the fastest. They are healthy, growing and need our products." Said another sales leader, "Value-oriented customers demand more from our company, but are willing to pay a premium in return. So, in the end, they are worth the effort."

The value segment is big. It is profitable. And it is growing. Executives at the Alexander Group's 2013 Spring Forum series generally agree on this point: If you want to achieve sustainable growth, then you need to focus on value selling.

What Type of Company Should Consider Value Selling?

Value selling may not be for every company, but it can play a role in the growth plans for more businesses than you might expect. Consider the following graphic which explores the relationship between value selling, product line complexity and product line breadth.

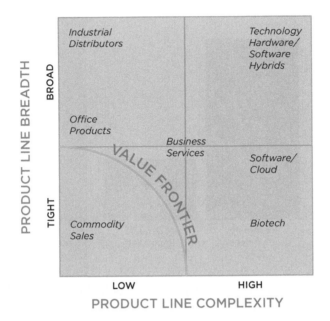

In this model, companies above the "value frontier," which have sufficient product line complexity and/or breadth, should seriously consider value selling in their growth strategy.

For instance, where product line breadth and complexity are *both* high as in the upper-right quadrant (think technology hardware/software/service hybrids such as IBM, HP), the opportunity to deliver value is robust. Such companies can help their customers conceive and implement processes that can improve either business efficiency (such as inventory control) or competitive advantage (such as customer information on demand for the sales force). These are the obvious places to build a value-sales capability. But it is far from the only place where *value selling* applies.

Companies in the upper-left quadrant, such as industrial distributors, carry relatively simple products but offer a vast array of them. Product line breadth spells an opportunity to help customers improve inventory management and working capital. For instance, innovative distributors offer inventory control services that cut inventory carrying costs in return for greater share of the business. The distributor has expertise in supply/inventory management, which they bundle with the products they deliver. The package enables sellers to talk process, ROI...and drag specific products along in the wake of this value-laden message. Product breadth can be leveraged to help customers become more *efficient*.

Similarly, companies with narrow but very complex product lines can also build value-selling capability. Biotech companies, for instance, carry relatively narrow but extremely complex product lines. Such innovative products can literally change healthcare outcomes and disease management models at the medical facilities in which they are used. This offers the seller a chance to teach customers how to innovatively leverage advanced features to improve business (or in this case, patient) outcomes. Product complexity can help customers become more *effective*.

Value selling can be applied to many different businesses. Either broad or complex product lines offer the opportunity to creatively identify ways to help customers improve their businesses and results. Where products and services can be used to improve customer business outcomes, value selling can be used to compete and win.

Where Does Value Selling Resonate?

Not all customers seek value from their vendors. Targeting those that do is vital to the effectiveness of a value-based growth strategy. Too often, targeting strategies use account size as the primary means of differentiation. Yet, account size does not necessarily correlate with appreciation for vendors who deliver value. In fact, the opposite is often true; large companies frequently try to intimidate their vendors into discounts. Value selling means bringing more assets to bear (skilled account managers, product specialists, application specialists, solutions specialists, product specialists, vertical specialists, etc.), so the cost of sales is high. Accounts that are targeted for such coverage must also appreciate value, and be willing to pay for it.

These important factors indicate whether an account is value-oriented:

- *Loyalty.* Does the account tend to stay with one company, or does it often switch vendors for better pricing? Repeat customers demonstrate by their behavior that they have a tendency not to shift over price alone.
- *Diversity.* Does the account buy a diverse basket of products and services, or do they "cherry-pick" based on price? Customers who buy multiple products from one vendor tend to define value beyond simple discounts.
- *Decisions.* Does the decision-making loop include general or functional executives who care about efficiency and effectiveness? If so, then value messages are more likely to resonate.
- *Risk.* How important is the purchase to the account? Will success or failure of the product affect their income statement... or is the purchase simply a rounding error? The more risk the customer assumes in the purchase, the more likely it is that value messages will resonate.
- *Strategy.* How does the customer compete in their own market? What words do they use to describe what makes them different? Are they avowed value sellers themselves, or do they compete on price? Companies that compete on value tend to buy based on value.

How are these factors assessed and integrated into a value-selling strategy? Knowing what customers value and segmenting them accordingly is not the responsibility of one organization...

it is a combined effort between product development, marketing, sales and service. The following diagram illustrates the emerging relationship between these functions:

1. New *social media* functions under the marketing umbrella gather and analyze unstructured data about target accounts and buyers to uncover emerging trends, insights and opportunities.
2. The *field marketing* function provides both planning and operational capabilities to produce alignment between marketing and sales, resulting in better tactical support.
3. Insights from both field and inside sales teams regarding account likes, needs and frustrations are accumulated by *field marketing* and passed along to product development for upstream planning purposes, and to sales, for immediate targeting.
4. More systematic interaction between *sales and service* (and, ultimately, marketing) is occurring to better leverage respected service representatives who resolve account issues, but who can also tactfully identify and pass along new opportunities to the sales function. Service resources help assess loyalty.

Finding and targeting accounts that are willing to pay a premium for value is serious business. The importance of this task is changing how traditional functions work together and is producing some entirely new functions (e.g., field marketing, social media marketing). Discovering where to focus value-selling resources is key to consistent and profitable growth, and new cross-functional teamwork is essential to achieving this capability.

Can You Deliver Value Through Sales at a Profit?

Four critical factors enable companies to deliver value-added services to profitably differentiate their offerings. They are *discrimination, depth, delivery and devotion*; or the "four Ds."

Discrimination

It is necessary to discriminate between accounts that are open to value messaging and those that simply covet discounts. Value-oriented accounts warrant more intense coverage. Price-oriented accounts do not. Kevin Hooper, senior vice president, Enterprise Platform Solutions at NEC Corporation of America, said, "I want 100 percent share of customers who want *me* to help *them* make money." Intense coverage of price-oriented accounts wastes resources that could have been deployed elsewhere to produce a better return on investment. Most companies cannot afford such waste. They need to discriminate and differentiate coverage according to what accounts value.

The coverage pattern emerging among sales organizations that discriminate where they deploy value-added resources is described in the following diagram:

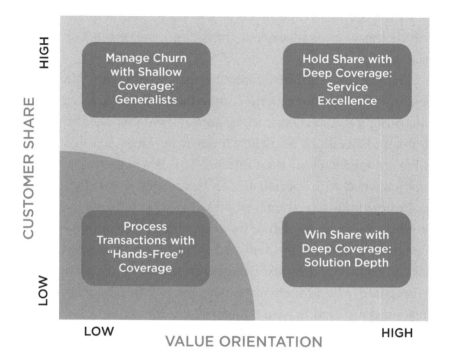

The dimensions that factor most heavily into coverage decisions (in addition to size) are an assessment of a) the customer's value orientation and b) the share of the business at the account. Where customer share is high but the value orientation is low (upper left), a fair amount of business is subject to switching for the right price. It is volatile. Such accounts warrant frequent but "shallow" coverage from generalists, perhaps even over the phone. In the lower left, where both customer share and value orientation are low, the trick is to cover the market efficiently with some combination of inside sales, website and/or partners. The goal is to attract a fair share of this transactional new business, as cheaply as possible.

In the upper right, both value orientation and customer share are high. These are your best current accounts. These are the customers on which you lavish specialists in the interest of maintaining and enhancing what is already a strong and (hopefully) profitable relationship.

In the lower right are the accounts that have a high-value orientation, but which are loyal to the competition. These are accounts that value insight and solutions…which are now being supplied by another company. Price alone won't lure them away. These accounts need a value message to pique their interest. This is where expert hunters, supplemented with specialists, can be targeted to good effect. The goal is to win these accounts when something changes (ownership, products, business model) or the competition errs and provides an "opening." These accounts will switch only to a viable contender that has earned the opportunity. Value-centric sales organizations should be prepared to build such relationships slowly and thoroughly; such customers are hard to win, but worth it in the end.

Below a certain level of value orientation and share (lower left), it may not be worth investing in direct coverage at all. Here, using the Internet, partners or (at most) inside sales may be the best way to provide coverage. Efficiency, not effectiveness, is the key to making money in this low-value segment.

Of course, the size of the account matters as well and should be factored into the equation. Paying attention to which accounts place value on insight and expertise helps sales leaders focus their scarce resources where they matter the most. This discrimination avoids pursuing procurement-centric RFPs at accounts (large and small) where sales expertise is not factored into the decision process.

Depth

Beyond knowing which accounts care about value, sellers need to understand the customer's business at a level that permits discussion about "how to do things better." According to 70 percent of executives polled at the 2013 Spring Forums, these accounts ascribe the greatest value to insights that help them generate more revenue.

Three things can pivot a sales organization away from transaction selling and attract value-centric accounts.

1. *Organize to turn insights into impact.* Companies are building whole new sub-functions within marketing to learn what customers value and to turn this into service overlays and messages for the sales organization. EBay has built a separate function nestled between sales and marketing known as the "strategic insights group," which mines unstructured social media data to produce a constant stream of insights about what customers are thinking and what they value. This group teams with marketing and sales to build segment sales strategies and help sellers prepare for sales calls. This distinctly cross-functional group feeds product development with ideas based on knowing what is on the customer's mind.

Other companies place the sales and marketing functions under a common executive. This better aligns their mutual interests and actions, while also beefing up resources in the field marketing team to enhance the ability to execute.

The common point is that leading companies are supplying sales with a steady stream of compelling insights and stories to support interactions at value-centric accounts. They are teaming multiple customer-centric functions (strategic marketing, product marketing, field marketing, sales and service) to maximize the value of their unique expertise.

2. *There is power in the story.* Value selling depends on targeting commerce leaders at the customers who care about the business, the balance sheet and the income statement. However, you only get one chance with these executives, so sellers need to be prepared when the opportunity is presented. They must be rock solid on the unique and compelling value they offer. Compelling cases or customer stories can help show how their offerings help businesses run better. Stories from the same vertical or related industries enhance the power of

the message; they confer instant credibility. As an added enhancement, great stories delivered by sellers who are teamed with their *own* top executive from sales, marketing or finance, add gravitas to the discussion and carry more weight.

3. *Delivering value means a longer sales process.* A value-centric sales culture can mean it takes longer to get to yes. One executive indicated, "You need to be able to bring the customer an insight, a trend, a fact that they can use to make money. When they make money, we make money. But this generally means a longer sales cycle." This is not accomplished with a short, highly efficient process. The sales process that delivers insights and process improvement is a longer one. Embrace it. Invest the time to find the issues that matter. Examine and choose the solutions that will have impact. Bring the customer something they can't do on their own. Then make up for the time invested by selling bigger, more profitable deals.

Dave Spencer, chief operating officer, East Sales of SAP, said, "If the seller does not add value to the sales process, then the process is quite short. Buyers do a lot of research on product up front and bring their own facts to the table. We need to add and leverage insight to be successful." David Phillips, president & chief operating officer of Yorktel, added, "If we can consistently solve customer problems, we can surf in a large account for years without getting slingshotted back to purchasing, which is the kiss of death." Matt Donnelly, vice president, U.S. Sales & Marketing-Patient Monitoring at Covidien, built on this by saying, "If we can drive the conversation to decreasing the length of patient stay, lowering overall procedure cost and lowering patient recidivism," then the seller has a business case to discuss with general management and can minimize the power of procurement in the decision-making process. None of this is accomplished quickly. Business cases take time to build. Executive relationships require careful construction. But the payback, better deals over a long period of time, is well worth it.

Delivery

Customer-facing resources, both sales and service, must be dedicated to helping clients implement the solutions that were sold. Sales organizations that succeed at value selling know that good stories need to be backed up by action and the capability to help the customer realize the promised ROI on their investment. Three dimensions of the sales function's increasing commitment to delivery are most critical:

- *No more siloes.* If you want an organization that can stand behind its promises and deliver value, then "no more siloes" is your motto. The sales function is no longer an island. Sales, marketing, product development and service functions, which have traditionally been run in separate siloes, are combining their resources and wisdom to deliver the value that customers demand. As Kathy Chou, vice president, sales operations and strategy at Intuit, nicely stated, "A co-dependency between these functions needs to be developed."

    This is accomplished through organization, planning and metrics. For example, eBay has placed sales and customer service under a common executive in Europe and North America. While the organizations remain separate, the new general managers have built common planning, metrics and coordinated processes to keep these two groups aligned. Customer support keeps a sharp eye out for opportunity, while sales promotes the full spectrum of products and services, from discovery to implementation, in one powerful voice. Nicholas Illidge, vice president, managing director merchant development at eBay International AG, said, "While you do not want to turn your service organization into sellers, you do want them to be a part of the sales discussion."

- *Skin in the game.* Some companies are putting their money behind their promises by crafting deals where higher margins are available only if the customer achieves the ROI originally discussed. In one example, an executive from the healthcare industry described how her company supplies product and service to select customers at a steep discount before the launch of new products (when such discounts are most needed) in return for better pricing after the new products have scaled and become more profitable. This is the inverse of deals where customers hammer suppliers for discounts once scale is achieved. In this model, the supplier takes risk up-front in return for enhanced margin downstream.

- *Attitude.* Kevin Hooper, senior vice president, Enterprise Platform Solutions at NEC Corporation of America, said it best with this observation: "Our sellers need to understand that success is not driven by just numbers. It is founded on extremely satisfied customers." In the value segment, reputation is maintained and enhanced by sellers and companies that over-deliver. This attitude is built on the belief that "the numbers will follow if you accumulate customers who value and appreciate what you have delivered." Customers first, numbers second.

Devotion

In the world of value selling, there is no "sell and run." If vendors want to be treated like partners, they need to show an unprecedented level of devotion to the client after the sale. There are several notable examples:

A nuanced role for the account manager. Account managers who are devoted to customer success play a critical role in helping customers realize the promised ROI. They balance the need to deliver results to the customer with the need to deliver results to their company. They do this by...

- Working more closely with service personnel.
- Accepting the role of the coach among service resources to enhance the overall customer experience and improve lead flow.
- Going deeper at a shorter list of assigned accounts with better relationships among higher level executives.
- Using past successes to create new opportunities; no more "aggressive waiting."
- Leveraging new media as a way to maintain contact with and stay informed about clients.

In other words, these account managers take the word "manager" in their title very seriously.

Help from marketing. The best value organizations create a marketing and sales team that do more together than they could separately. Examples abound. At eBay, leadership teamed marketing and sales to analyze and garner insight from customer Net Promoter scores. Marketing now uses the scores and comments to identify which customers loved and hated what. They work with sales to rapidly change or eliminate identified sources of friction and to scale the practices identified as most valuable. As another executive nicely stated, they have "woven marketing and sales seamlessly into the customer coverage process."

Emerging importance of social media. Sellers in the value segment are beginning to see the value in social media as a way to not only stay connected with clients but as a way to learn about their ongoing challenges and thinking. New media does not replace in-person dialog, but it can help alert sellers to emerging issues (sometimes with the help of friends in marketing). Used well, social media can help identify opportunities and arm the account manager with relevant insight before the call.

A Word About Culture

In the value-centric company, product development, marketing, sales and service have a shared purpose: customer success. This implies cross-functional interlock in areas such as planning, coverage, organization, job design, metrics and compensation. Value selling is the opposite of "sell and run." It is what some executives are beginning to call "accountability coverage," where the sales function is responsible for the whole customer contact continuum, from discovery to implementation to results. This means finding ways to work smoothly across multiple functions that share this mission, this mania for customer success. When it comes to the customer, these functions must speak the same language and share a common culture.

Every sales leader agrees: Nothing happens in the transformation to value selling (or anything else for that matter) until the first-line sales manager (FLSM) helps redirect the sales culture. If you are planning to transform your sales organization to a value platform, you must consider the role of this critical position and get these field leaders invested. Here's how:

- Train the trainers on what value means and their role as a centerpiece of the transformation. Help them understand the role of the sales organization in delivering value.
- Help FLSMs become better coaches is a sound investment, which can ensure that training concepts translate into action. Ninety percent of training (or more) is forgotten unless sellers are required to put the new tools into play and are coached on their performance.

- In the transformation process, it is critical for managers and sellers alike to hear from the customer...what do they expect of a value-centric sales force? FLSMs need to get into the field. Sometimes it helps to assign them an account to keep them current. This field-level insight should be reflected in the planning process and the actions of their sellers.
- Empowerment is key. Let the FLSMs know that they are crucial to the success of the transformation. Give them the authority to represent the new culture in the field. Ask them to assess their people in a new context. Give them the latitude to make a difference.

Closing Comments

Value selling is not for everyone. The breadth and complexity of the product line needs to fit. It takes time and investment to set up. It may not deliver results right away. And pulling cross-functional teams and processes together is hard work. But as one executive noted, "Value selling requires you to think like a customer. When you do this, you see the world very differently. And that can open up a whole new world of possibilities."

This customer- and value-centric viewpoint is central to enabling both the company and the seller to shift from product pushing to being a true "partner in commerce" with the customer. In an age when value means competitive advantage, companies need to think very carefully about whether and how to develop a version of *value selling* that works for them.

Chapter 20

Make Change Your Secret Weapon

Author:
Gary S. Tubridy
Senior Vice President
The Alexander Group, Inc.

AT A RECENT SUMMIT attended by 12 top sales executives, the subject of discussion was: In an age of extraordinary volatility, how can leaders equip their sales organizations to adapt so quickly and effectively that the ability to change becomes a competitive advantage?

The sales leaders in attendance agreed on three points:

- *Customers are demanding more value.* Whether it is deeper discounts, more insight or better support, today's customers want more from their vendors.
- *Sales leaders depend on the successful delivery of value-added growth strategies.* The sales force is at the heart of most of these. To succeed, sellers must be able to deliver and often implement the insights that add precious value to the products they represent.

- *Many sales leaders struggle to implement such value strategies.* Sales forces are often not ready or willing to adopt the more complex sales processes that increasingly sophisticated customers expect.

Most importantly, sales organizations need to move faster... much faster.

Sales organizations that can quickly adapt will be the winners. Achieving consistent sales excellence is no longer just about a one-time transformation to address customer needs at a point in time. Market and customer volatility is now a way of life. Year-over-year sales growth depends on the sales organization's ability to see and respond to opportunities quickly and consistently. Successful leaders will not wait for change to be forced on them; they will seek it out.

This paper offers top-line insight distilled from the Summit discussion on how sales leaders can hone the ability of their organizations to embrace change and act swiftly. Observations fell into the following categories:

MANAGEMENT PHILOSOPHY	KEY CHALLENGE
It is better to change from a position of strength than desperation?	What are the early signs that change is needed?
Expect that most people will resist change.	How do you position change in a positive light?
Never expect sellers to simply figure it out.	What tools enable sellers to change successfully?
When managing in permanent white water, change is a way of life.	What steps can you take to create a change-friendly culture?

Management Philosophy: It is better to change from a position of strength than desperation.

Key Challenge: What are the early signs that change is needed?

Forward-thinking sales executives seek "headlights" into a critical question: When will change be needed? They want advance warning, time to plan. Historical sales trends often do not tell the whole story. If you wait for a sign that change is needed to appear in your numbers (e.g., market share decline), you have likely waited too long. What else can you look for? Summit participants recommend the following:

- *For early warning, you have to look outside the company.* External factors to watch include new regulations, new technologies, even new competitors. But watching even these variables is much the same as reacting to what someone else is doing… you just get earlier warning. Perhaps the best source of "early warning insight" is getting to know what customers value that you are not currently providing…but could. To do this well, a strong marketing and sales partnership is needed, leveraging marketing's ability to analyze/conceptualize with the sales function's access to customer insight.
- *Make it a habit to make customers your co-creator of change.* Bring the client into the center of developing the need for and elements of change. Bring the ecosystem of your company into this co-creation. Marketing and product development need to hear about what the client needs from the client's mouth. Customers have ideas. Sellers have access. Marketers have skills. Mix it all together and add a little customer urgency and you have a powerful, action-oriented early warning system.

- *Watch the actions of your sales force.* This will help to a) gauge the consistency of their actions with your strategy and b) determine if you are getting quality execution. Top executives need to know whether their sellers are:
    - Calling on the right accounts and buyers.
    - Delivering the right messages.
    - Executing new sales protocols in a quality fashion.

Acquire this insight through front-line sales manager observation, customer input, sales time tracking or some combination of all three. Look at time allocation and behaviors critically and early in your fiscal year. Be prepared to act in the first quarter; if you wait for more definitive results, you will have waited too long.

Management Philosophy: Expect that most people will resist change.

Key Challenge: How do you position change in a positive light?

It is no mystery that change, particularly big change, scares most people. They resist it in favor of continuing to travel more comfortable, known paths in their assigned accounts and geographies. Yet, there are exceptions to this rule; indeed in some organizations change is expected and individuals are always ready, even eager for it. How do these organizations do it? Participants described a four-part process that they feel can maximize an organization's willingness to change:

- *Give them the big picture.* Tell sellers they are part of something big, something designed to make both them and the organization successful, even unique. Just about every good seller wants to be associated with a winning organization and culture. Give them a window into the big strategic picture. Show them how the changes are designed to keep their organization on top by providing what customers want and doing it better than the competition.

- *Show what is in it for them.* Get specific about how individual sellers can gain by participating in and leveraging the change. Use all the levers: more sales, better compensation, recognition, career development. Maybe even better work/family balance. Show both the short- and long-term perspectives; prove that change can be rewarding to those who do it well.
- *Create momentum.* Don't ask everyone to be a pioneer. Find the thought leaders. Sell them on the change strategy first. Perhaps involve them in a pilot to learn more through their insightful feedback. Convert these field leaders into "change acolytes." Give them opportunities to put the word out and give the expected change their stamp of approval.
- *Communicate frequently.* Don't try to do it all in one big presentation. Show the big picture. Then keep the news flowing by reporting progress and successes. Celebrate individuals who deserve it. Be careful to solicit questions from the field. Use first-line managers to accumulate issues and distribute answers. Create a regular column on your sales intranet… "great questions, great answers." Put simply, consider communications a process not an event.

One participant cautioned against using the term "pilot," because it implies you might not fully implement. Instead, use the terms Wave 1 and Wave 2. You learn in Wave 1 and adjust in Wave 2, but like the ocean the waves keep coming. There is no going back.

Make it clear that you do not expect sellers to do more. Change is not accretive. If you ask sellers to do something new, you also need to be clear about what you want them to stop doing. If you don't make that choice, then the sellers will make it for you. That means consciously deleting responsibilities, anything from call points to under-producing accounts and segments. Such decisions can lead to healthy tension with product marketing executives, who will want to protect their hard won share. But in a world of limited resources, choices must be made. Sales executives need to be leaders in this decision process, not mere consumers of it. Find new ways to cover low-growth accounts and markets. Deploy expensive sellers where they can make a difference.

Management Philosophy: Never expect sellers to simply "figure it out."
Key Challenge: What tools enable sellers to change successfully?

Of course, sellers need to be equipped to handle change. But don't think about this as simply a training issue. While training is a part of the solution, Summit participants uniformly advise that sellers need stronger "real-time" guidance and clarity about what is expected.

Sales processes are more complex these days, involving sellers in more parts of the "ecosystem." To succeed in change on this scale, sellers need access to playbooks. Such playbooks should:

- Describe the new selling situations, as well as the sales processes associated with each; call points, cadence, messages, etc.
- For each process, identify resources and expertise available to assist in the most complex situations.
- Be readily available. Consider committing such playbooks to newly available cloud software services to make this guidance available to sellers on demand.

Next, consider how to motivate sellers to do things differently. No one wants to try something new and fail, so sales leaders need to help them succeed. Here are some thoughts Summit participants shared on how to do this:

- Do not underestimate the difference between selling to middle management (most common) and selling to higher level executives (more desirable and important today). At minimum, executive selling requires training on the basics of finance and the language of ROI. As well, some insight into relevant business processes and approaches to process improvement is recommended.

- If you do nothing else, train your first-line managers on the new processes you are implementing. Give them the tools to critique and coach their sellers toward excellence. If you sell your line managers on change, the rest will soon follow.
- If you have run pilots or "waves," document one or several success stories in cases that offer detail on sales process as well as outcomes. Don't forget about the importance of accumulating customer references. Nothing convinces a seller faster than another seller's satisfied customer. If possible, put cases on the website and let sellers post questions to the author of the case for even deeper insight.

Management Philosophy: When managing in permanent white water, change is a way of life.

Key Challenge: What steps can you take to create a change-friendly culture?

Sales executives must make change a way of life. Too often, the reverse is true. Often, the parts of the organization that have never had to change are always the least willing to accept change. Many support people have never been in front of a client. Don't let that be the case in your organization. Instead make your sales force "a vital organism, not a museum." Teach the organization to expect change through the following actions:

- *Frequently bring change to them.* Sometimes it is big, like an important new product. Sometimes it is smaller, perhaps a minor addition to the compensation plan. But do not let sellers get comfortable with "the way things are done around here."
- *Make the effort to keep sellers in the know.* Communications make it all work. Don't cut back on communications resources; they

are vital in an ever-changing environment. Sellers can deal with a lot if you simply clue them in on what you want and why.

- *Articulate how change is connected to the growth strategy.* Give change a solid strategic foundation by aligning what you are asking sellers to do with some important aspect of the growth plan. Let sellers know that what you are asking them to do is meaningful.

In the final analysis, the imperative to manage the sales function through constant change and improvement is the responsibility of sales leadership. Leaders who display "healthy paranoia" by always looking over their shoulder and never being satisfied and who are a combination of "innovative and demanding," are indeed central to the success of top performing sales organizations.

But these sales leaders need one more thing. The missing ingredient, so often overlooked, is the ability to transmit the need for change throughout the organization. Sales leaders at this Summit offered insight into techniques they use to get their sellers and managers on board with the change imperative, to transform from selling things to selling value. If that is the path you are on, and change is on your agenda, consider these insights in your planning for 2013.

Chapter 21

Navigating the Transformation to Value Selling

Author:
Gary S. Tubridy
Senior Vice President
The Alexander Group, Inc.

THE ALEXANDER GROUP (AGI) conducted two Regional Forums at which six keynote speakers explored what it takes to compete and win in today's economy of tight budgets and increasingly sophisticated buyers who demand ever more value.

These keynote speakers described mission-critical transformations undertaken to move their sales forces from "transaction engines" to "value providers." Much was learned about the mechanics of a successful transformation such as customer segmentation, messaging, job and organization design, infrastructure, etc., but the most valuable insights dwelt on the cultural and political aspects of managing a successful transformation.

- How do you prepare an organization for change?

- How do you get stakeholders excited about it?
- How do you get traction for change when most sellers find it scary?

AGI learned how the speakers gave their transformation plans the heart and soul needed to animate them, to move successfully from the drawing board into the field. As one executive stated, "You cannot 'tell' change. You have to convert the change imperative into personal action."

This executive summary provides insight into what sales leaders must do to ignite a transformation mandate and manage the ensuing transformation process. Findings are divided into two categories:

Sage advice on how to ignite a transformation mandate. Some words of wisdom that keynote speakers had for their peers who may be wondering where to start and how hard to push a transformation. Words that prompted one leader attending the conference to say, "I wish I had heard this before I started my own sales transformation."

Managing the politics of transformation management. Interested parties need to be lined up and their support secured if meaningful transformation is to be accomplished. The speakers offered advice on which groups to enlist and what to ask of them.

Sage Advice on How to Ignite a Transformation Mandate

"My vision was to build a value-added selling strategy that aligned with changing customer needs and captured more share of the market."

This comment came from one speaker who went on to admit that the 2008 recession had catalyzed a turning point for his business. Change was not an option. The question was where to begin?

It was neither a time to freeze up nor a time to panic. It was time to seek opportunity by changing in ways that made the company more attractive than the competition.

As a whole, the speakers assessed the situation and galvanized action. They did so methodically, enthusiastically and with a positive attitude, recognizing that their ability to change quickly and meaningfully was a real advantage. This ignited the transformation mandate in their organizations. Following is some of their sage advice on how to make this happen in your company.

- *Start from the outside and work your way in.* Said one executive, "You have to answer two basic questions: What do your customers want that no-one else is offering, and how can you deliver that better than the next guy?" Our speakers were each fixated on learning what customers needed (sometimes even before the customer realized it) and figuring out how to provide it through sales coverage excellence.
- *Know your capabilities deficit.* According to one speaker, "To succeed, you must focus not only on what you are good at. You need also to find what you are not good at and determine whether this is important to customers. If it is, you better chart a course for improvement." Assess what is important to customers and size the gap in your ability to deliver it. Know what you cannot do and whether it is worth doing. Develop a plan for you and your sellers to win the *new* game...don't gear up to win the last war with an improved version of yesterday's capabilities.
- *Lift people up...don't kick them along.* Don't threaten people into change. Take the opposite tack. Congratulate them for their past success. Entice them by offering an opportunity to, as one executive stated, "be great again." Explain why the path toward greatness means everyone from the CEO on down

must embark on a value-driven change journey. Describe the journey and offer them a choice…the choice to take part in it.

- *Lay the foundations for a culture of mutual accountability.* Said one executive, "Each seller must understand that their failure or success creates broad ripples." Sellers, managers, the whole team needs to understand and act from a belief in the importance of their individual contributions. They need to act not because they are "being watched," but rather because the team is counting on them. These executives are leveraging something that the military has long known… that individuals will adapt and sacrifice for the good of the team if they believe in the mission and know that the team is counting on them.

- *Make value your chief ambition.* In the words of one executive, "Sales used to be all about 'more'…more sellers, more calls, more transactions. Today, the 'more' we are most concerned about is 'more value'." In that vein, another executive paraphrased Albert Einstein: "Strive not to be a success but, rather, to be of value." Make being a member of your team contingent on giving customers better insight and helping them improve how they manage their businesses.

- *Hurry, but don't rush.* Despite the urgency of change, our speakers made it clear that panic is not an option. Don't rush and never "change for the sake of changing." Said one executive, "Take care to observe, ask questions and learn the facts. Understand what your customers do and what they want. Learn who they are buying from and why. And, importantly, why not you?" Commit to action only when you have the insight to win.

Build the case. Make the case to your team. Commit to value. Have a plan. Good advice from leaders who have met and mastered the transformation challenge.

Managing the Politics of Transformation Management

"Successful transformation is animated by alignment of thinking and commitment to action up, down and across the organization."

This same executive also said, "I'd rather have a good plan well executed than a great one that never made it off the drawing board." These executives were impressive in how they handled the technical side of their transformations. They knew that their best bet to thrive in the new economy was to transform from selling things to selling value. And, as illustrated in the following chart, they knew that to do so they would need to transform their approach to segmentation, channels to market, job design, metrics, compensation and talent.

But there was something else these executives knew about a successful transformation, something missing from the above diagram. They knew that nothing would really change until all the relevant interest groups were aligned and pulling in the same direction. As illustrated below, these executives were careful to overlay the technical transformation process with careful planning to align the interests of five critical interest groups: *top management, sales management, marketing, sellers* and, last but not least, *customers.*

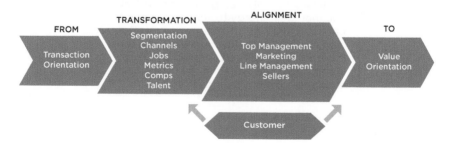

The keynote speakers at this Regional Forum made transformation a priority by taking great care to ensure that it was also a priority among these key interest groups. Their success hinged on a change management approach that at once set direction, aligned resources, enabled action and assessed outcomes. All of them took steps to embrace each group by clarifying its role in and contribution to a successful transformation process. They also took the time to define the benefits that would accrue from a successful transformation. Key findings are summarized below:

INTEREST GROUP	WHAT SALES LEADERSHIP ASKS OF THEM	AND PROMISES IN RETURN
Top Management	Sales leadership sees to it that top management not only participates in the sales transformation journey, it helps chart the course. True, transformation plans need rock solid grounding in the numbers; costs, benefits, returns and time frames must all be addressed. The transformation has to make good business sense. But at companies that get sales transformation right, there is a deep understanding that it requires investment, time, persistence and a belief that it is the right thing to do to get and keep competitive advantage in this post-recession economy. Sales leaders make sure that top management knows that the value delivered to the customer through the sales process is indeed a part of the product. Said one executive, "Top management respects the importance of sellers and takes steps to capture and channel their energy to serving the needs of customers." Another commented, "Top management sets the course and the tone; it both challenges and enables sellers to step up to transformation that helps our customers benefit their customers."	Sustainable, profitable sales growth & share gain.

INTEREST GROUP	WHAT SALES LEADERSHIP ASKS OF THEM	AND PROMISES IN RETURN
	Transformation to customer-motivated value selling isn't some scheme cooked up by the VP of Sales as the latest "strategy de jour." It is driven from the top down, shared across the organization and is a core part of the company's marketing strategy and value system.	
Sales Management	Leadership challenges sales management to embrace the role of coach and mentor and to invest time and energy to transform sellers from transaction generators to value engines. There is explicit acknowledgment of the line manager's critical role to the success of the organization, even of the company. This challenge is backed up by investments designed to help line managers succeed in this transition, including: • Training on how to be an effective manager in transformation. Companies provide options from "Line Manager Boot Camp" to "Value University." • Detailed playbooks providing the line managers with instructions, tools and insight into what they need to do differently and why. • Sales funnel management templates that integrate longer and more complex sales processes with "customer discovery" guidelines, detailing what the manager should expect sellers to understand about each solution opportunity. • Innovative assessment protocols designed to promote "improvement instead of 'gotcha' management." Notably one executive described how they used top performing line managers to conduct periodic peer reviews of other districts as a way to "root out poor practice and export best practice."	Shared prominence and greater recognition for marketing's role in delivering profitable growth by improving competitive positioning.

INTEREST GROUP	WHAT SALES LEADERSHIP ASKS OF THEM	AND PROMISES IN RETURN
Marketing	Sales leadership offers to partner with marketing to enable deeper understanding of not only what customers need but what they really value. Marketing and sales team up to package products and services into the kind of value-based solutions that position the company as a premium provider to value-conscious decision makers at the highest levels of the customer hierarchy. One sales leader paraphrased the edict that his CEO laid out for the sales and marketing team: "Get and keep customers by delivering products and services that they value." In this company, marketing planning and sales execution are not done in sequence; they are done in parallel with marketing and sales tightly interlocked as initiatives are launched, assessed, refined and re-launched. Said one executive, "Clarity about what the marketing and sales team is expected to do and deliver as a team relieves common tensions between these two organizations." Examples of such teamwork include: • Seller wisdom is used by marketing to shape research initiatives and is integrated into research findings to help turn customer comments into insights that inform marketing strategy. • Sales expertise is used by marketing to develop sales pitches that integrate expertise on differential product features and customer business processes to create messages that are "both compelling and very difficult for the competition to match." The partnership is enabled by a communications protocol that regularly intersects sales and marketing resources to "better plan, execute and assess sales campaigns" that leverage product, industry and solution variances.	Shared prominence and greater recognition for marketing's role in delivering profitable growth by improving competitive positioning.

INTEREST GROUP	WHAT SALES LEADERSHIP ASKS OF THEM	AND PROMISES IN RETURN
Sellers	One of our speakers noted his belief that "customers should view the seller as the smartest person in the room when it comes to understanding issues and proposing solution alternatives." Sellers need to know that this is what is expected. And they need to understand the professional rewards, both monetary and intrinsic, that will accrue to them for achieving this position. The assistance they received to build their solution selling skills arsenal was significant: • A highly articulated "discovery process that gets every seller behaving like an entrepreneur while delivering value at a consistent level of quality." Sales leaders count on such processes to help sellers develop deep understanding of a) strategies and outcomes the customer is counting on, b) plans they have in place to support this and c) showstoppers that could get in the way. This amounts to what one executive called "thoughtful questioning and active listening leading to deep understanding." • Tools devoted to giving sellers the opportunity to acquire and deliver relevant expertise to the customer. Such tools included online databases of industry solutions and competitive positioning, hardware such as iPads to enable easy access to data and even virtual access to noted experts in particular solutions or technologies. • Targeted training and coaching from first- or second-line managers and a supervisory model that gives sellers credit for excellence in delivering value to their customers.	Shared prominence and greater recognition for the role of sales in delivering profitable growth by improving competitive positioning.

As well, these sales leaders were careful to build a pipeline of direct feedback from customers to the sales organization, enabling efficient and unvarnished assessment of the transformation effort. Said one speaker, "The pipeline to the customer helps us learn what is working, what is not and enables careful and appropriate recalibration," minimizing tendencies to backslide into old patterns of behavior.

INTEREST GROUP	WHAT SALES LEADERSHIP ASKS OF THEM	AND PROMISES IN RETURN
Customers	Sales leaders appeal directly to customers for feedback, exhorting them to participate in surveys and communicate their thinking on outcomes and value. Said one executive, "If you can't measure it, you should not bother doing it." Measuring impact on customer attitudes on value delivered is, in the words of another executive, "as critical as the sales results." These sales leaders made it a point to do customer research with an eye toward both confirming value delivered and learning how to deliver more of it. To be sure, marketing is a partner in conducting this research. But make no mistake, sales executives are consumers and users of insights derived. Our speakers recounted efforts to: • Acquire broad survey research into whether particular customers would recommend their company to others… the net promoter metric…to get an overall assessment of value delivery as well as specific insights into which customers were especially pleased…and which were not. • In-depth research into companies and customers that were especially happy or especially dissatisfied to better understand which practices to scale and which to change or discard.	Improved service, more reliable partnership and deeper insight into potentially game changing ways to run the business.

INTEREST GROUP	WHAT SALES LEADERSHIP ASKS OF THEM	AND PROMISES IN RETURN
	At the end of the day, said one executive, "We try to find pockets of brilliance where we are doing things that can be institutionalized." Said another, "In their planning, we try to get all our sellers focused on what they need to do to add value to the customer. Period. All the numbers are relegated to the appendix." This same executive is not bashful in saying, "You must sometimes force your sellers to think about the customer...but after a while it is second nature."	

Closing Comments

What is the takeaway here? First, if your sales team is not adding value, it is headed to extinction. Sales forces that do not add value cannot compete with low-cost distribution channels such as the Internet.

Second, the journey to adding value usually requires a transformation in both capabilities and attitude. Skin-deep reorganizations do not amp the ability of a sales organization to bring solutions to customers.

And third, sales executives driving a transformation process frequently underestimate the importance and the difficulty of transforming attitudes about the role and value of the sales force.

A sales organization with a value mandate cannot be built or run in isolation. Careful management of multiple stakeholder groups is needed to produce the lasting changes in attitude that a successful transformation demands. If you want your sellers to add value, you have to add value to your sellers. This is not an argument for higher levels of sales compensation.

Our speakers argued that top management, middle management and peer organizations must all recognize the critical role of the seller in differentiating from the competition, winning business and driving profitable growth. This is more true than ever if you are asking the sales organization to up its game and increase its prominence in the marketing mix.

Transformation is not only about strategy. It's also about winning hearts and minds both in and outside of the sales organization. Pay attention to both strategy and the human element, plan to both respect and inspire and a successful transformation to value selling can be yours.

Appendix

Participating Companies:

American Express
Avaya
Avon
Bausch & Lomb
Becton Dickinson
Blue Coat Systems
Boston Scientific
CA Technologies
CenturyLink
CDW Corporation
Cisco Systems
CitationShares Holdings
Columbia Business School
Covidien
DJO
Deluxe
Demand Media
eBay
EFI
Epicor
Equisales

Experian
FedEx
GE Healthcare
Hearth & Home Technologies
Hewlett-Packard
IBM
Ingersoll Rand
Intercall
Intuit
Lifetouch
McAfee
Medtronic
Merrill
Monster
Motorola Enterprise Mobility
NEC Corp. of America
Pearson Education
Pentax Medical
Perkin Elmer
Pfizer
Pitney Bowes

Polycom

Riverbed

SAP

Siemens Healthcare Diagnostics

Siemens PLM

Sigma-Aldrich

Thomson Reuters-Americas

Thomson Reuters

Time Warner Cable

UPS

WebMD Health Corporation

WorkflowOne

World Kitchen

Xerox

Xerox Global Services

Yahoo!

Yorktel

About Alexander Group

The Alexander Group (www.alexandergroup.com) provides sales management consulting services to the world's leading sales organizations, serving Global 2000 companies from across all industries. Founded in 1985, Alexander Group combines deep experience, a proven methodology and data-driven insights to help sales leaders anticipate change, align their sales force with company goals and make better informed decisions with one goal in mind—to grow sales. The Alexander Group has offices in Atlanta, Chicago, San Francisco, Scottsdale and Stamford.

Our Consulting Services

The Alexander Group provides the world's leading sales organizations with management consulting services for the full spectrum of sales force needs, as well as compensation analysis and performance benchmarking based on the industry's richest repository of sales data.

We apply years of experience and our Sales Management System™, a proven methodology for evaluating sales organizations, to provide insights that are rooted in facts. We not only deliver insights—we understand sales and marketing business challenges. We roll up our sleeves to work alongside our clients, whether they are slightly realigning their sales coverage model or radically overhauling their sales force. Beyond that, our keen focus on measurement ensures that we deliver value to our clients. And results.

About Alexander Group Events
Produced by sales professionals for sales and marketing leaders

The Alexander Group produces and facilitates a specialized portfolio of events that help the world's leading sales organizations drive growth. From the Chief Sales Executive Forums to Executive Roundtable conference calls, all events cover topics that range from big-picture strategy to hands-on execution. Participants benefit from connecting with other top sales and marketing leaders, and gain exclusive access to the latest ideas and deeper insights needed to create high-performance sales organizations.

About the Author

GARY S. TUBRIDY is a senior vice president with the Alexander Group, and the general manager in charge of the Firm's management consulting business. He is located in Stamford, Conn. Gary's consulting work is focused on increasing marketing and sales effectiveness with particular emphasis on technology and medical products companies. He has personally managed projects in sales organization design, sales force sizing and deployment, sales performance management and sales compensation design.

Gary has deep functional expertise in diagnosing sales management issues and helping clients execute action plans to improve results. He is currently researching and chronicling best practices of leading sales organizations in North America and enjoys organizing events specifically for top sales executives, including the Chief Sales Executive Forum. He is one of three founding stockholders of the Alexander Group.

CPSIA information can be obtained at www.ICGtesting.com
Printed in the USA
BVOW11s2041290414

352091BV00007B/20/P

9 780989 948067